Via Airmail

An Aerophilatelic Survey of Events, Routes, and Rates

Edited by
Simine Short
with
Cheryl Ganz, Associate Editor

The American Air Mail Society

Chicago 1992

SPECIAL NOTICE

Library of Congress Cataloging-in-Publication Data

Via Airmail: an aerophilatelic survey of events, routes, and rates / edited by
   Simine Short, with Cheryl Ganz, associate editor
   224 p.
   Includes bibliographical references.
   ISBN 0-939429-01-2 (hardcover)
   1. Airmail service--History. 2. Postage-stamps--Topics--Airmail service--
History. I. Short, Simine, 1944-. II. Ganz, Cheryl. III. American Air Mail Society.
HE6238.V53   1992
769.56"49383144--dc20   92-53852
                                                                        CIP

Printed by Edwards Brothers, Ann Arbor, Michigan, United States of America.

Contents

American Air Mail Society

Organized 1923 as the Aero Philatelic Society of America

Foreword

Aerophilately has many aspects. The aim of this book is to show you the numerous fields of airmail collecting.

Aerophilately is the study of the development of airmail services and the collection of documents pertinent to such development.

A flown cover may tell you about the history of aviation, the development of postal history, the success (or failure) of postal air transportation or the usage of postage stamps or even machine meter markings. Thus, aerophilately is also an integral part of philately with all its aspects.

May this book help the collector to understand what aerophilately represents. May it also help find new friends of our hobby which is — in our opinion — the most rewarding and wonderful hobby in the world.

May I, as President of FISA, the International Federation of Aerophilatelic Societies, express my sincere thanks to those who worked hard to make this publication possible.

Roland F. Kohl
President, FISA

Preface

The first all-airmail stamp exhibition sanctioned by the American Philatelic Society, is being held in Chicago during CHICAGOPEX '92. At the same time, the American Air Mail Society (AAMS), the International Federation of Aerophilatelic Societies (FISA), the Aerophilatelic Federation of the Americas (AFA) and the Space Unit Study Group are holding their annual meeting or convention. Several other major aerophilatelic societies from the United States and Canada are also participating.

This book, *Via Airmail*, presents a cross-section through aerophilately which we hope will appeal to philatelists from all disciplines. The seventeen articles in this book cover the past one hundred and twenty years. Aerophilatelic events, flights, pilots, airlines, and airmail postage rates are surveyed. In-depth research is presented which may open up opportunities for additional research.

The American Air Mail Society continues its practice of publishing new aerophilatelic research. This book will, we hope, be the beginning of a new concept for the Society, to periodically publish a compendium of articles which are too short for a book and too specialized to be used in the *Airpost Journal,* the monthly publication of the Society.

The success of this project depended on a team effort. The *Aerophilately 1992* committee was formed in 1987, with Stephen Neulander as Chair. Five other aerophilatelists were actively involved not only in assembling this book but also in making the CHICAGOPEX '92 all-airmail exhibition a full success. These members were Raymond Broms (Chicago Air Mail Society President and AFA Liaison), Cheryl Ganz (Associate Editor and Chicago Philatelic Society Liaison), Robert Outlaw (AAMS Liaison), Dr. Reuben Ramkissoon (Space Unit ATA President and APS Liaison), and Simine Short (FISA Liaison and Editor).

Most of all, we want to thank the authors of the seventeen articles published in this book. Because dedicated aerophilatelists like these have devoted time to write and share their research, we feel this book will be of value to the reader and their work will promote the aerophilately of the future.

In an editorial in the September 1991 *Air Post Journal,* editor Jim Graue spoke of aerophilately: "The development of airmail, from the exotic beginnings to the common carrier of today, is an area rich in philatelic potential, much of which is yet to be explored. We are challenged to show these (new) collectors the significance, fascination and challenges of aerophilately. ... (aerophilately) is an area with a wide spectrum of subjects and approaches. It has something for everyone, and we must become agents for it."

We hope you enjoy reading and using this book. We also hope that you share your research with others so that you, too, become an agent for aerophilately.

Simine Short
Editor, *Via Airmail*
Fall 1992

Introduction

AMERIPEX '86, the international stamp exhibition held in Chicago in 1986, was the largest philatelic event in American history. It attracted conventions of all of the major airmail organizations, including the American Air Mail Society, the International Federation of Aerophilatelic Societies and the Aerophilatelic Federation of the Americas.

Chicago aerophilatelists bonded together with an enthusiasm to continue the cooperative efforts and two concepts emerged. The first idea was to hold an all-airmail exhibition in the United States recognized by the American Philatelic Society as a national rated show. An *Aerophilately 1992* committee was formed. The Chicago Philatelic Society agreed to host this airmail exhibition during CHICAGOPEX '92. The second was a publication to share the knowledge that some collectors had spent years studying. This aerophilatelic survey should appeal to beginning and advanced collectors of airmail as well as to postal historians and other philatelists.

We hope that you enjoy reading in these pages of the aviation and aerophilatelic events from Chicago and beyond, spanning the beginnings of airmail to more recent events. In future years, we hope that you will refer to this book many times as a reference source offering rate and route information not readily available in any other single document.

Enjoy!

Cheryl Ganz
Associate Editor, *Via Airmail*
President, American Air Mail Society

Acknowledgements

The American Air Mail Society, supported by its Memorial Publication Fund, encourages research and publication of airmail related subjects. The 1988-1989 Board of the AAMS gave its blessing to the idea to publish anthologies or compendiums periodically in the future. The AAMS Publication Committee, chaired by Allen D. Jones, gave guidelines for the production of the book.

Many people gave ideas and suggestions in the process of creating *Via Airmail*. A very special thanks goes to Robert Outlaw, past-president of the American Air Mail Society. He was AAMS liason and middleman between the AAMS, the editors, and the printer. He was always available with help, and advice.

We were fortunate in having Jeannette and Jim Adams edit the manuscript while it was still in the beginning stages.

Editorial help came from Charles J. Peterson of the APS Writers Unit who checked and found several instances where clarification by the authors was warranted. His input was surely appreciated.

Bill Welch, editor of the American Philatelist, was always a telephone call away when technical (and other) advice was needed. His input, just prior to the manuscript going to press, was of utmost value. He, as the professional, noticed—among other items—a few "spacing problems," created by the software, which were corrected.

Numerous other experts read and edited specific articles for accuracy and presentation. All these efforts helped a great deal.

For the record, the manuscript was created on a Mac IIsi with WordPerfect (vers 2.04). The book was printed by Edward Brothers, Inc. using postscript files.

1

United States

Domestic

Airmail Rates

by James R. Adams

The intent of this article is to give the collector of United States domestic airmail a source of easy to use rate charts. The tables contain all information needed to determine the rates of domestic cards and covers. A text giving historical background information is provided so that the collector may better understand the effect of the historical settings on the rating structure.

This article will treat the complete development of United States airmail rates from the forerunner period until domestic rates ceased in 1977.

The term "post card" is used throughout this article to encompass postal cards (those issued by the government) as well as post cards (privately printed cards, frequently but not always picture cards).

In the beginning: The Forerunners

In 1877, a private stamp was issued for the flight of the *Buffalo* Balloon from Nashville, Tennessee. Although this was a private venture, 5 cents were charged for the vignette (stamp). All mail carried on the flights still required United States postage for further transmission within the postal system.

Figure 1: Envelope with the 5-cent *Buffalo* balloon vignette, addressed to Shohola, Pennsylvania (from *Catalog of Classic American Airposts and Aeronautica, 1784-1900*).

With the first flight of a heavier than air ship by the Wright brothers on December 17, 1903, the way was opened for airmail transmission. By 1910, a prize of $50,000 was offered by William Randolph Hearst for anyone who could fly across America in 30 days. On September 17, 1911, Calbraith Rodgers took off from Sheepshead Bay race track on Long Island, New York. Rodgers arrived at Long Beach, California, on December 10, 1911. Due to the length of time of the flight, he did not win the $50,000 prize. However, during the flight, 25-cent private labels were issued to be affixed to post cards and flown by Rodgers to the next stop. The post office still required official postage to be affixed for further transmission.

The Pioneer Period: 1911 - 1916

During this period a number of flights took place at various events such as fairs and aviation meets. Between September 23 and October 1, 1911, the first "official" airmail was flown in the United States during the Garden City, New York, Air Meet. Mail was flown from the Air Meet grounds and dropped to the Postmaster at Mineola, New York. On September 23, 1911, Earle L. Ovington was sworn in as "First Aeroplane Mail Carrier in the Post Office of the United States." Although the Post Office Department was assigning airmail route numbers to these flights, letters and cards were still required to be carried at the regular surface rates. Figure 2 shows a cover with the 2-cent letter rate, autographed by Earle Ovington, the first United States airmail pilot to be sworn-in.

Regulations prohibited an additional charge for air service on post office authorized flights.

Figure 2: September 1911. First official airmail in the United States. Earle O. Ovington, first American airmail pilot. to be sworn-in.

The Governmental Period: May 15, 1918 - June 29, 1924

With the entry of the United States into World War I on April 6, 1917, most aviation was directed toward the war effort.

The Post Office Department, with an appropriation of $100,000, established an experimental air route from Washington to New York with an intermediate stop at Philadelphia to exchange mail and planes. The War Department agreed to furnish both planes and pilots.

On May 15, 1918, the first experimental route opened. A special bi-color 24-cent airmail stamp was issued to pay the air rate plus special delivery.

Figure 3: First Day of rate — world's first scheduled airmail service, using Army pilots and planes: New York—Philadelphia—Washington.

On July 15, 1918, the rate was lowered to 16 cents with special delivery still being included. Since the reduced rate was scheduled to take place on July 15, 1918, one would expect the last day of the 24-cent rate to be July 14, a Sunday. There was no airmail flown on Sundays during 1918. As a consequence, a last day of rate cover would have to be postmarked on July 13, Saturday.

On August 12, 1918, the flying of mail was taken over by the Post Office Department with its own planes and pilots.

Figure 4: Second day of rate — 16 cents per ounce rate; special delivery service was still included.

On December 15, 1918, the rate was changed to 6 cents and special delivery was no longer included. A new 6-cent airmail stamp was issued.

On July 18, 1919, formal domestic airmail was discontinued.

Starting on this day, first class mail was flown for the normal surface rate while the transcontinental air route was being developed. After the inauguration of the transcontinental air route, first class letter mail was forwarded by air until June 29, 1924.

United States Domestic Airmail Rates

PIONEER and GOVERNMENTAL PERIOD

1911 - 1924

PIONEER PERIOD 1911 - 1916	No additional fee for airmail, same as surface rate 2¢ per ounce for letters 1¢ per ounce for **un**sealed letters 1¢ post card rate
GOVERNMENTAL PERIOD May 15, 1918 - July 13, 1918	Washington — Philadelphia — New York 24¢ per ounce or fraction thereof; special delivery was included. 24¢ post card rate
July 15, 1918 - December 14, 1918	16¢ per ounce or fraction thereof; special delivery was included 16¢ post card rate
December 15, 1918 - July 17, 1919	6¢ per ounce or fraction thereof; special delivery was **no longer** included 6¢ post card rate
FORMAL AIRMAIL DISCONTINUED July 18, 1919 - June 29, 1924	2¢ per ounce or fraction thereof; rate same as first class. Airmail carried on space available basis at normal surface rate: 2¢ per ounce for letters, 1¢ for cards 1¢ post card rate

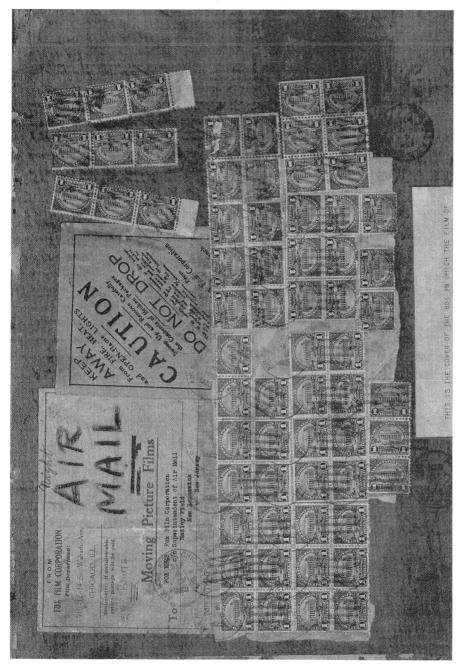

Figure 5: This is the cover of the wooden box in which the film documenting the wreck of the airship *Shenandoah* was shipped to Fox News.

Government Zone — Contract Period:
June 30, 1924 - January 31, 1927

On June 30, 1924, the Post Office opened the transcontinental route. The route had been planned and tested for several years. The three zones were New York to Chicago, Chicago to Cheyenne, and Cheyenne to San Francisco. The availability of a beacon lighted airway contributed to the feasibility of an effective transcontinental airmail scheme. Three new airmail stamps were issued to pay the new zone rates of 8 cents, 16 cents, and 24 cents.

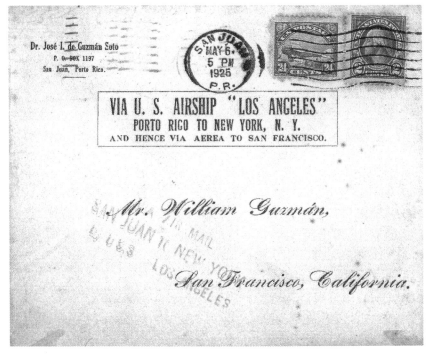

Figure 6: 24 cents postage was required for airmail service on the transcontinental route.

Because of the amount of commerce in Chicago and New York City, the need for a fast overnight handling of the mail from these two major cities was evident. On July 1, 1925, an overnight airmail was inaugurated. An additional 2 cents premium over the zone day rate of 8 cents was charged for this service.

United States Domestic Airmail Rates

GOVERNMENT ZONE — CONTRACT PERIOD

June 30, 1924 - January 31, 1927

GOVERNMENT ZONE RATE: Three Zones June 30, 1924 - January 31, 1927	New York — Chicago; Chicago — Cheyenne; Cheyenne — San Francisco 8¢ per ounce or fraction thereof, per zone or part of zone 8¢ post card rate per zone or part of zone
OVERNIGHT GOVERNMENT ZONE RATE New York — Chicago Zone **only** July 1, 1925 - January 31, 1927	New York — Chicago (both directions) intermediate stops: Bellefonte, Pennsylvania; Bryan, Ohio; Cleveland, Ohio 10¢ per ounce or fraction thereof 10¢ post card rate
CONTRACT AIRMAIL RATES February 15, 1926 - January 31, 1927	Per ounce or fraction thereof 10¢ on routes not exceeding 1,000 miles 15¢ on routes exceeding 1,000 miles, but not over 1,500 miles 20¢ on routes exceeding 1,500 miles * post cards rate same as letter rate

* Although this rate existed, no route exceeded this distance during the rate period

Contract Airmail Rates:
February 15, 1926 - January 31, 1927

The Post Office Department invited bids from private carriers for various airmail routes. These routes were to connect with the already existing government routes. From this beginning, commercial aviation in the United States was born and supported by airmail subsidies. A 10-cent airmail stamp was issued to pay the rate for one contract route of not more than 1,000 miles. On February 15, 1926, the first such contract went to the Ford Motor Company. Two Contract Airmail routes, CAM No. 6 and CAM No. 7, were opened between Detroit and Cleveland and Detroit and Chicago. These routes were flown by planes of the Ford Motor Company.

On April 15, 1926, CAM No. 2, a route from St. Louis to Chicago was opened by Robertson Aircraft Corporation. Robertson's chief pilot was a young ex-Army flyer by the name of Charles A. Lindbergh (Figure 7). Lindbergh was sworn in as "carrier of the mails" on April 13, 1926, just thirteen months before he was to fly into international fame for his solo trans-Atlantic flight.

Later in 1926, an airmail stamp of 15 cents was issued to pay the rate for routes over 1,000 miles, but less than 1,500 miles. The only contract route that was over 1,000 miles was from Seattle to Los Angeles.

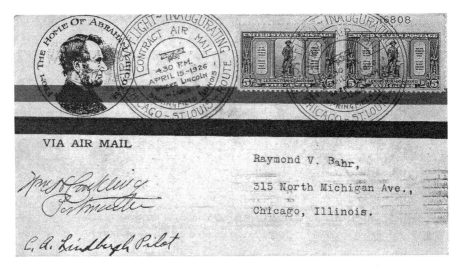

Figure 7: 10-cent Contract rate for service on private contract carrier route, pilot Charles A. Lindbergh.

Combination Government Zone — Contract Period: February 15, 1926 - January 31, 1927

This period was one of the most confusing for United States rates. An effort has been made in this section to simplify the rate structure. The sixteen CAM routes listed here are the **only** possible routes to interact, rate wise, with the Government Zones. The Government Zone rates were reduced to 5 cents per zone when flown in conjunction with one or more CAM routes. The single letter rate was 10 cents for **each** CAM route flown.

An example is a letter from Los Angeles, California, to Rochester, Minnesota on December 24, 1926. (Figure 8). After April 17, 1926, the CAM from Los Angeles connected with the transcontinental route at Salt Lake City, Utah. The rate for this CAM was 10 cents. Next came one partial and one full Government Zone, each at the reduced rate of 5 cents per zone (Governmental routes Salt Lake City to Cheyenne, and Cheyenne to Chicago). On June 7, 1926, the CAM between Chicago and Minneapolis opened up. The CAM rate for this leg was 10 cents. Thus, the airmail postage for a letter from Los Angeles to Rochester was 30 cents.

Figure 8: Contract route Los Angeles — Salt Lake City; Government route over two zones Salt Lake City—Chicago; Contract route Chicago—St Paul.

United States Domestic Airmail Rates

Combination:

GOVERNMENT ZONE — CONTRACT PERIOD

February 15, 1926 - January 31, 1927

COMBINATION GOVERNMENT and CONTRACT PERIOD	Government Zone Rate per Zone when used with one or more Contract Routes
February 15, 1926- January 31, 1927	5¢ per ounce or fraction thereof per zone post card rate same as letter rate
February 15, 1926- January 31, 1927	Contract Rates per **each** Contract Route or partial route flown, per ounce or fraction thereof 10¢ on routes not exceeding 1,000 miles 15¢ on routes exceeding 1,000 miles, but not exceeding 1,500 miles post card rate same as letter rate.

Combination: GOVERNMENT ZONE and CONTRACT PERIOD
These Contract Routes are the ONLY Routes that figure in the Combination Rates.

February 15, 1926 - January 31, 1927

First Flight	Route #	Route, with Intermediate Stops
Feb 15, 1926	CAM 6	Detroit, MI —Cleveland, OH (Dearborn,MI)
Feb 15, 1926	CAM 7	Detroit, MI — Chicago, IL (Dearborn, MI)
Apr 1, 1926	CAM 10	Jacksonville, FL — Miami, FL (Tampa, FL, via Ft. Myers, FL)
Apr 6, 1926	CAM 5	Elko, NV — Pasco, WA (Boise, ID)
Apr 15, 1926	CAM 2	Chicago, IL — St.Louis, MO (Peoria, IL, via Springfield, IL)
Apr 17, 1926	CAM 4	Salt Lake City, UT — Los Angeles, CA (Las Vegas, NV)
May 12, 1926	CAM 3	Chicago, IL — Dallas, TX (via Moline, IL , St. Joseph, MO, Kansas City, MO, Wichita, KS, Oklahoma City, OK, Ft. Worth, TX)
May 31, 1926	CAM 12	Cheyenne, WY — Pueblo, CO (Denver, CO, via Colorado Springs, CO)
Jun 7, 1926	CAM 9	Chicago, IL — Minneapolis, MN (Milwaukee,WI, via LaCrosse, WI, via St. Paul, MN)
Jul 1, 1926	CAM 1	New York, NY —Boston,MA (Hartford,CT)
Jul 6, 1926	CAM 13	Philadelphia, PA — Washington, DC

Special Service to the National Air Races (for one week only) Sep 4 to

Sep 11, 1926	CAM 13	Philadelphia, PA — New York, NY (Washington, DC)
Sep 15, 1926	CAM 10	Atlanta, GA — Miami, FL (Macon, GA inbound to Jacksonville, FL, via Tampa, FL, via Ft. Myers, FL)
Sep 15, 1926	CAM 8 [*]	Seattle, WA — Los Angeles, CA (Portland, OR, via Medford, OR, via San Francisco, CA, via Fresno, CA, via Bakersfield, CA)
Sep 27, 1926	CAM 10	Macon, GA: First dispatches from this city.
Oct 1, 1926	CAM 5	Change of terminal from Elko, NV, to Salt Lake City, UT
Oct 10, 1926	CAM 15	Philadelphia, PA — Norfolk, VA (Washington, DC)

* Only route to require the 15-cent rate: Seattle, Washington, to Los Angeles, California, 1,099 miles.

Uniform Rate Period:
February 1, 1927 - June 30, 1934

The rates changed to a uniform rate structure on February 1, 1927. One of the changes was that the rate was now based on each half ounce, not per full ounce as in previous rate periods. The uniform rate applied both to Government and Contract Routes, one rate for anywhere within the United States.

On January 25, 1927, a new 20-cent airmail stamp was issued to pay the double letter rate.

On June 30, 1927, the Post Office Department ceased to fly any of the airmail routes.

Beginning July 1, 1927, all airmail in the United States was flown by private contractors.

Figure 9: Last day of Uniform Rate—10 cents for half ounce. A new stamp was issued for the 5 cents rate.

Figure 10: Domestic 5-cent rate for first ounce, and 10 cents for each additional ounce.

Again on August 1, 1928, the airmail rate changed to 5 cents for the first ounce. The second ounce or fraction thereof was 10 cents (see Figure 10). This was the first time that the rate for the second rate increment was higher. A 5-cent airmail stamp was issued to pay the first ounce rate.

On July 6, 1932, a new rate took effect. The rate of 8 cents for the first ounce and 13 cents for each additional ounce went into effect. An 8-cent stamp was issued for this rate in September 1932.

An important event took place during this rate period. On short notice, President Roosevelt canceled all airmail contracts, effective February 19, 1934. Between February 19 and 21, 1934, the United States Army Air Corps flew the mail over the main routes. Because of the many mishaps, the public reaction was one of shock. The routes were quickly renegotiated. The McKellar-Black Airmail Bill authorized the return of all airmail transportation to private air carriers, subject to meeting certain qualifications.

The private contractors again took over the flying of the mails. The new contracts specified the routes as Air Mail Routes (AM). The Post Office revised the entire route setup and renumbered them. There were no more CAM routes.

United States Domestic Airmail Rates

UNIFORM RATE PERIOD

February 1, 1927 - June 30, 1934

UNIFORM RATE PERIOD Rate applied to both Contract and Government Routes February 1, 1927 - July 31, 1928	Per **half** ounce or fraction thereof 10¢ for the first half ounce and each additional half ounce or fraction thereof post card rate same as letter rate (20¢ for DOUBLE rate letter)
5¢ RATE PERIOD August 1, 1928 - July 5, 1932	Per ounce or fraction thereof 5¢ for the **first** ounce 10¢ for each **additional** ounce post card rate same as letter rate (15¢ for DOUBLE letter rate)
8¢ RATE PERIOD July 6, 1932 - June 30, 1934	Per ounce or fraction thereof 8¢ for the **first** ounce 13¢ for each **additional** ounce post card rate same as letter rate (21¢ for DOUBLE letter rate)

Figure 11: Double rate — 15 cents for a double rate letter. United States airmail used as 10 cents postage due and 6 cents paid in Hawaii for airmail coast to coast..

Figure 12: 8 cents rate for first ounce, 13 cents for each additional ounce or fraction thereof.

6 cents and 8 cents Period:
July 1, 1934 - September 30, 1946

With the rate change on July 1, 1934, the basic rate was again 6 cents per ounce or fraction of one ounce. The aircraft industry was now expanding and building larger aircraft. With these advancements came larger pay loads of passengers, freight, and mail. The airline industry was growing and service became more dependable.

One event of importance that occurred during this rate period was the National Air Mail Week celebration of 1938. This was an idea of United States Postmaster James A. Farley to promote the use of and publicize domestic airmail by the general public. In later years, Farley would say he felt that the National Air Mail Week 1938 was one of his greatest successes because airmail became generally accepted by the public.

On March 26, 1944, a new airmail rate began. With the United States at war, the new rate included an unusual provision. The rate of 8 cents **per ounce** applied to civilians as well as members of the Armed Forces within this country.

Also on March 26, 1944, the rate to and from members of the Armed Forces **outside** the United States remained the same at 6 cents **per half ounce**. This rate was somewhat of a domestic rate as it applied to mail addressed to stateside A.P.O.s.

As of April 1, 1944, for the first time, airmail postage was included on official penalty mail. The United States Congress voted to allow airmail postage free on ballots for the election of 1944. Members of the Armed Forces were granted free airmail postage for returning their war ballots to local election officials.

Figure 13: Two different "War Ballots." They were allowed to be mailed by airmail, free.

United States Domestic Airmail Rates

6 cents and 8 cents Period

July 1, 1934 - September 30, 1946

6¢ RATE PERIOD
 	
July 1, 1934 -
  March 25, 1944
	6¢ per each ounce or fraction
	  thereof
	post card rate same as letter rate
	
	(12¢ for DOUBLE letter rate)

8¢ WAR RATE PERIOD
War rate applied to civilian
  and Armed Forces personnel
  INSIDE the continental
  United States
 	
March 26, 1944 -
  September 30, 1946
	8¢ for each ounce or fraction
	  thereof
	post card rate same as
	  letter rate
	
	(16¢ for DOUBLE letter rate)

6¢ WAR RATE PERIOD
6¢ war rate applied to mail sent
  by or to Armed Forces
  personnel **OUTSIDE** the
  continental United States.
 	
March 26, 1944 -
  September 30, 1946
	Per **half ounce** or fraction
	  thereof
	
	6¢ for first half ounce and each
	  additional ounce or fraction
	  thereof
	post card rate same as
	  letter rate
	
	(12¢ for DOUBLE letter rate)

FREE WAR BALLOT
First time penalty mail has
  airmail postage free. For the
  elections of 1944 ballots to or
  from members of the armed
  forces received free airmail
  service.
U.S. Congress votes to allow
  as of April 1, 1944
	No Weight Restrictions on
	  War Ballots
	
	Free airmail service for war
	  ballots

5 cents and 6 cents Period:
October 1, 1946 - July 31, 1958

With the end of World War II, domestic commercial aviation began to grow and expand. In 1946, the airmail rates were returned to the pre-war rates.

In 1949, the rates were again reduced. The number of cities served by commercial flights was growing. Also, for the first time, airmail postal or post cards had a different rate from letter rates.

United States Domestic Airmail Rates

5 cents and 6 cents Period

October 1, 1946 - July 31, 1958

5¢ RATE PERIOD
 	
October 1, 1946 -
   December 31, 1948
	5¢ for each ounce or fraction
	   thereof
	post card rate same as
	   letter rate
	
	(10¢ for DOUBLE letter rate)

6¢ RATE PERIOD
 	
January 1, 1949 -
   July 31, 1958
	6¢ for each ounce or fraction
	   thereof
	4¢ post card rate
	
	(12¢ for DOUBLE letter rate)

7 cents, 8 cents, and 10 cents Period:
August 1, 1958 - May 15, 1971

During the rate periods between 1958 and 1971, domestic airlines expanded their route network and began using jet aircraft extensively.

The airmail rates were on the increase along with first class rates.

United States Domestic Airmail Rates

7 cents, 8 cents, and 10 cents Period

August 1, 1958 - May 15, 1971

7¢ RATE PERIOD
 	
August 1, 1958 -
  January 6, 1963
	7¢ for each ounce or fraction
	  thereof
	5¢ post card rate
	
	(14¢ for DOUBLE letter rate)

8¢ RATE PERIOD
 	
January 7, 1963 -
  January 6, 1968
	8¢ for each ounce or fraction
	  thereof
	6¢ post card rate
	
	(16¢ for DOUBLE letter rate)

10¢ RATE PERIOD
 	
January 7, 1968 -
  May 15, 1971
	10¢ for each ounce or fraction
	  thereof
	8¢ post card rate
	
	(20¢ for DOUBLE letter rate)

11 cents and 13 cents Period:
May 16, 1971 - October 10, 1975

In the years between 1971 and 1975, the United States Postal Service handled an increasing volume of mail of all classes. A larger volume of airmail needed to be handled as well. With the extensive system of daily flights, the United States Postal Service began looking at the possibility of carrying all classes of mail by air for speed and efficiency.

United States Domestic Airmail Rates

11 cents and 13 cents Period

May 16, 1971 - October 10, 1975

11¢ RATE PERIOD
 	
May 16, 1971 -
  March 1, 1974
	11¢ for each ounce or fraction
	  thereof
	9¢ post card rate
	
	(22¢ for DOUBLE letter rate)

13¢ RATE PERIOD
 	
March 2, 1974 -
  October 10, 1975
	3¢ for each ounce or fraction
	  thereof
	11¢ post card rate
	
	(26¢ for DOUBLE letter rate)

10 cents, 13 cents, and 17 cents Period: October 11, 1975 - May 1, 1977

Starting on October 11, 1975, the United States Postal Service announced that all first class mail would be upgraded to the same service as airmail. A separate airmail rate ceased to exist, all mail was handled at the first class rate.

On December 28, 1975, the first class (airmail) rate was again increased.

Also on December 28, 1975, a new domestic airmail rate was established. There were two reasons for this rate change. First class mail could not be insured, but airmail could be insured. With an airmail rate again in effect, this class of mail was now insurable. The second reason was the fact that Mexico would not handle by air any mail from this country that did not have an airmail surcharge. When this rate ended on May 1, 1977, first class mail could be insured, and Mexico agreed to handle United States first class mail by air without an airmail surcharge.

Figure 14: Special airmail rate — 17 cents for airmail service plus 60 cents for insured mail.

United States Domestic Airmail Rates

10 cents, 13 cents, and 17 cents Period

October 11, 1975 - May 1, 1977

10¢ RATE PERIOD U.S. Postal Service upgraded first class mail to same service as domestic airmail — first class mail flew as airmail October 11, 1975 - December 27, 1975	10¢ per ounce or fraction thereof 7¢ post card rate (20¢ for DOUBLE letter rate)
13¢ RATE PERIOD First class rates changed : First class mail moved by air First class rate was in essence air rate December 28, 1975	13¢ for the **first** ounce 11¢ for each **additional** ounce 9¢ post card rate (24¢ for DOUBLE letter rate)
SPECIAL AIRMAIL RATE 17¢ RATE PERIOD Air rates had utility only for sending insured mail by air and providing a legal base for an airmail rate to Mexico. After May 1,1977, first class mail could be insured and Mexico agreed to handle U.S. first class mail by air without airmail surcharge December 28, 1975 - May 1, 1977	17¢ for the **first** ounce 15¢ for each **additional** ounce 14¢ post card rate (32¢ for DOUBLE letter rate)

Conclusion

Two different domestic services that are not covered in this article are Airmail Parcel Post and Express Mail. While both these services are part of the domestic airmail service, these rates are outside the scope of this study.

Hopefully, the information supplied in this article with its accompanying charts will be of help to collectors in determining the correct postage rate for cards and covers in their collections. The collecting of rate covers and associated postal history can be a fascinating part of aerophilately.

Bibliography:

Silver, Philip. 1977. "United States Domestic Air Mail Rate Changes First and Last Days." *American Air Mail Catalogue.* Vol 2 ed 5: 491-499. The American Airmail Society: Cinnaminson, New Jersey.

United States Post Office Department. *United States Official Postal Guide* July 1929. Government Printing Office: Washington, DC.

United States Post Office Department. *United States Official Postal Guide.* Government Printing Office: Washington, DC. Miscellaneous issues.

United States Post Office Department. *United States Official Postal Guide Monthly Supplements.* Government Printing Office: Washington, DC. Miscellaneous issues.

James R. Adams is a member of the Board of Directors of the American Air Mail Society and has served as its Secretary. He is a national rated philatelic judge and has won gold and special awards for several exhibits, including airmail rates. Jim is a past president and currently a board member of the Indiana Stamp Club, host society of the annual stamp exhibition INDYPEX. Other collecting interests include early New York postal history, British trans-Atlantic mail, military posts, Lindbergh, and National Air Mail Week.

2

Beacon

Airmail Rates to

Foreign Destinations

by **Kent J. Kobersteen**

Made possible by new technology and development in aircraft design, and spurred by dramatic pioneer flights such as Lindbergh's 1927 North Atlantic crossing, airmail service expanded rapidly throughout the world in the late 1920s.

During this period, aircraft began to span longer and longer distances, not only in the United States, but throughout the Caribbean, Central and South America, Europe, and parts of Asia and Africa.

Frequent rate and route changes were brought about by expanding and changing routes, changes in the economics of providing air service, and modifications to international postal agreements.

All of these factors make the relatively short period of use of the Beacon airmail stamp a very intense—and hence, fascinating—period of airmail activity. This same intensity, brought about by rapidly changing rates and routes, makes deciphering covers of this period often quite challenging. Contributing also to this challenge is the fact that few of the people who were posting airmail letters during the period understood the complicated rates. Nor should students of these covers assume that postal clerks figured rates with full and correct knowledge of the rate structure. One sees many more incorrectly franked covers than correctly franked ones.

This article examines airmail rates of the period of use of the United States Beacon airmail stamp—August 1928 through 1930—and shows as examples covers from the author's collection.

Domestic Rates

The Beacon airmail stamp was issued on July 25, 1928, to provide franking for a significant reduction in the airmail rate which was to become effective on August 1. The airmail rate was reduced on that date from 10 cents per half ounce to *5 cents for the first ounce and 10 cents for each additional ounce or fraction thereof.* There was no separate airmail postcard rate, hence no savings over a one ounce letter.

While the Post Office Department wanted to encourage the use of airmail by lowering the rate, it did not yet have the capacity to carry parcel post by air. To discourage the sending of heavier parcels and packages, the rate for each additional ounce was set at a rate higher than that of the first ounce.

Airmail to the Caribbean, Canal Zone and to Central and South America.

Although trans-Atlantic airmail was not yet available, airmail service in the Caribbean was expanding rapidly during this period. As a matter of fact, Lindbergh himself flew the airmail on numerous Pan American Airways routes in the Caribbean.

Even though service on these routes was direct from the United States, and no steamship transport was involved, when airmail service was inaugurated to some Caribbean points (Puerto Rico, Haiti, and the Dominican Republic), as well as the Canal Zone, the airmail rate was stated by the Post Office Department as being *in addition to regular postage.* Although these "in addition to regular postage" rates were in effect for only a short period — ten weeks in most cases — the confusion this wording caused was long-lasting.

The rate to Puerto Rico, the Dominican Republic and Haiti was 10 cents per half ounce in addition to the regular postage of 2 cents per ounce. Incidently, the rate for post cards was 10 cents in addition to the regular postage of 1 cent.

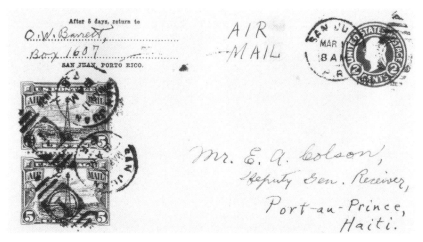

Figure 1: A cover from San Juan, Puerto Rico, to Port au Prince, Haiti, at the rate of 10 cents per half ounce plus the regular postage of 2 cents per ounce.

Figure 2: A double rate cover from the brief period when the rate from the United States to the Dominican Republic was 10 cents per half ounce plus the regular postage of 2 cents per ounce.

These rates were in effect from the date of inauguration of airmail service (January 9, 1929, for the Dominican Republic and Puerto Rico; January 21, 1929 for Haiti) until the rates were lowered to a straight 10 cents per half ounce on March 20, 1929.

When airmail service was inaugurated between Miami and the Canal Zone on February 4, 1929, the rate was 25 cents per half ounce plus the regular postage of 2 cents per ounce. On March 20, 1929, this rate was lowered to 25 cents per half ounce.

Covers posted during this short period, other than first flights, are quite unusual. Figure 1 is a cover posted in San Juan, Puerto Rico, on March 11, 1929, addressed to Port au Prince, Haiti. Figure 2 is a double-rate cover posted to the Dominican Republic at the rate of 10 cents per half ounce plus regular postage. Figure 3 shows a cover posted to the Canal Zone at the rate of 25 cents per half ounce plus the regular postage of 2 cents per ounce.

Figure 3: When airmail service was inaugurated between Miami, Florida, and the Canal Zone, the rate was 25 cents per half ounce plus the regular surface postage of 2 cents per ounce.

Airmail rates to Central and South American countries, on the Foreign Airmail Routes (which, during this period, were in the process of being inaugurated) are relatively complex but they are more straightforward than the short-lived "plus regular postage" rates discussed above.

Figure 4: A cover to El Salvador showing the rate of 15 cents per half ounce. The cover is marked for routing via Miami, Florida, on Foreign Air Mail Route 5, and is backstamped in San Salvador on July 4, 1930, and in La Libertad, El Salvador on July 5.

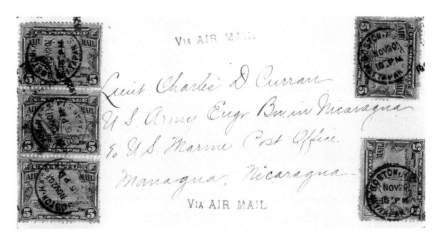

Figure 5: This cover was posted in Boston on November 20, 1929, during the period of the 25 cents per half ounce rate to Nicaragua.

These rates are listed in Table I (see pages 51-54). Rates are first date of rate, or date notice given of a rate change "effective immediately." Rates are per half ounce, or fraction thereof, unless otherwise noted.

Figure 4 shows a cover posted to El Salvador on June 28, 1930, bearing the correct postage for that period. Shown in Figure 5 is a cover to Nicaragua posted on November 20, 1929, at the rate of 25 cents per half ounce.

Domestic Air plus Steamer Service

In considering mail destined for Europe, or mail which was routed via Europe, one must remember that we are dealing here with a period a little more than a year after Lindbergh flew the Atlantic. Hence trans-Atlantic airmail was still nearly a decade away.

Most mail that went overseas travelled by steamship across the ocean, as it had for decades, although it might first be flown in the United States. Many postal patrons of the period (and collectors today) assumed that the domestic airmail rates applied for the air service within the United States. They did not.

Figure 6: Posted at Minneapolis on November 13, 1929, this cover bears both manuscript and rubber stamped markings indicating it is to be transported "Via London."

Letters going overseas were charged the normal surface rate—5 cents for the first ounce and 3 cents for each additional ounce, except to England, Spain and the Americas where the rate was 2 cents per ounce— plus a domestic airmail rate of *4 cents for the first ounce and 8 cents for each additional ounce, or fraction thereof.*

Thus, a one ounce letter going from Chicago to Paris would be properly charged 4 cents for the domestic airmail and 5 cents for the surface rate to France, for a total of 9 cents. A similar letter from Chicago to London would be charged 4 cents for domestic airmail and 2 cents for the surface rate to England, for a total of 6 cents.

Airmail from London and Paris

During the period under discussion, airmail service to Europe, parts of the Middle East, and the west coast of Africa, was available on numerous routes originating in London and/or Paris.

Covers to European destinations with air service provided on these routes are relatively common. Figure 6 shows a cover to Switzerland marked for air service "Via London." The rate was figured as 4 cents for United States internal airmail, 4 cents for airmail from London to Switzerland, and 5 cents for the surface rate, for a total of 13 cents.

To accurately decipher these rates and routes to European destinations it is essential to be familiar with the air services available on the European Continent. Table II (see pages 55-57) lists the air routes and their respective route numbers for the London to the Continent service as they were shown in the July 1929 *United States Postal Guide*, as well as the rates for service on these routes. Table III (see pages 58-59), from the same source, gives similar information for air routes from Paris.

This rate and route information was current at the time of publication of the July 1929 *United States Postal Guide*. Route information seemed to change significantly from year to year; rates changed less often, but they do vary. It is recommended that the serious student not only consult the appropriate *Postal Guide*, which was published each July, but also the monthly *Postal Guide Supplements*. The supplements provide news of rate and some route changes and give specific dates for the changes, but they also provide a wealth of additional useful information for the specialist.

Confronted with an airmail cover from the United States to a European country, the collector has the following options available by which the sender may have intended the cover to be transported:

- Airmail within the United States, surface mail to London or Paris, and by air to destination.
- Airmail within the United States, surface mail to destination.
- Surface mail within the United States, surface mail to London or Paris, and by air to destination.

The cover shown in Figure 7 was underpaid for air service on the route from Paris to Casablanca, Morocco, and hence received the marking "VIA AIR MAIL TO EXCHANGE OFFICE." The double bar rubber stamp was applied to indicate that the paid-for air service had been completed. In the United States, these were usually applied at the Exchange Office at Varick Street, New York City. This double bar rubber stamp marking was to signal to the foreign postal administration a "canceling" of the airmail notation. The sender had only paid for airmail within the United States.

Figure 7: This cover, from Chicago to Casablanca, was underpaid for air service from Paris to Morocco, received a "VIA AIRMAIL TO EXCHANGE OFFICE" marking at Chicago, and the double parallel bars to cancel the airmail at New York.

If the cover in question does not bear the double bar hand stamp, and one assumes it was correctly handled at the Exchange Office, one can deduce that payment was made for foreign air service.

If the rates do not "add up," the first thing to try is to see whether or not the rates would do so if the domestic air formula of 5/10 cents, rather than the correct 4/8 cents, were used. One must be aware that at this point one is entering into the realm of speculation. How can a person be sure that one rationale on the part of the postal patron of 60 years ago is more valid than another? One can not. The author feels it is very important that the collector qualify any statements which are made based on assumptions of this nature, when writing up a cover.

Thirty-five cents was the correct rate for the cover in Figure 8, which was figured as follows: 4 cents for airmail service within the United States (Cleveland to New York), 6 cents for air from Paris to Budapest, 5 cents for the surface rate to Budapest, and 20 cents for foreign special delivery.

Figure 8: Thirty-five cents was the correct rate on this cover posted in Cleveland on December 9, 1929. It arrived in Budapest on December 22. The cover received air service from Cleveland to New York and from Paris to Budapest.

The cover in Figure 9 bears the correct rate of 28 cents: airmail from Milwaukee to New York (4 cents), air from London to Germany (4 cents plus the surface rate of 5 cents) and 15 cents for registry.

Figure 9: This cover bears backstamps from Milwaukee on October 26, 1928, New York City on October 27, London on November 5, and Dresden on November 8 with correct rate of 28 cents for air service in the United States and Europe and for registry.

Figure 10 shows a "problem" cover which must be carefully written up in a collection or exhibit. This is one of those covers where no matter how one tries to figure the rates, the components never exactly add up to the franking on the cover. It is, nonetheless, an interesting usage.

This cover was posted in Fullerton, California, and addressed to Ootacamund, India. It shows the marking "Via London" and was forwarded to Bangalore, India. The rate is figured as follows: United States internal airmail at 4 cents for the first ounce, 8 cents for each additional ounce; London to India air service at 12 cents per half ounce plus the surface rate of 5 cents for the first ounce and 3 cents for each additional ounce; 15 cents for the registry fee with no additional indemnity available on international registered mail. This gives a total of 36 cents for a letter under half ounce, 48 cents for half to one ounce, and 71 cents for one to one and one half ounces. Because franking on this cover is 59 cents, one may assume that most likely the cover is an overpaid half to one ounce letter.

Figure 10: A classic "problem" cover for the student attempting to decipher rates. On this cover the assumption is that it is an overpaid half to one ounce envelope. The cover bears backstamps of Fullerton, California on December 8, 1928; New York on December 11; London on December 20; Ootacamund, India on January 7, 1929; and Bangalore, India on January 9.

Figure 11: This cover received air service only from London. It bears the correct rate of 5 cents to Germany, plus 4 cents for air service from London. The cover also bears a manuscript notation requesting air service from London and a Hamburg airmail receiving marking.

Figure 11 shows a cover from Baltimore with payment for foreign air service but not for domestic airmail. This cover was carried by rail from Baltimore to New York, via the steamship from New York to England, and airmail from London to Hamburg.

Not dealt with in this article is mail of the period which went via West Coast exchange offices to Asia, Australia, and the Pacific. Although there were air routes in service in these areas—most notably in China—covers originating in the United States and carried on these routes are very elusive.

As one delves deeper into the issues of rates and routes, studies the *Postal Guide* more thoroughly, and is fortunate enough to discover even more esoteric covers, one discovers that there were also special rates for air service in Belgian Congo—French Equatorial Africa, Peru, Colombia, and Australia. All of these are dealt with in the 1929 *Postal Guide,*

The subject of mail carried on SCADTA, the Colombian air service, is a complicated study in itself. Suffice it to say that covers bearing one or more SCADTA adhesives and United States airmail franking are quite unusual. Although they do exist in limited quantity, the subject is mentioned here "for the record" only. One such cover is shown in Figure 12.

Figure 12: Sociedad Colombo Alemana de Transportes Aereos, SCADTA, obtained concessions from a number of South American governments to carry the mail. This is a double rate cover bearing markings of Chicago, January 7, 1929; New York Varick Street, January 8; Cartagena, Colombia, January 19; and Bogota on January 22.

Figure 13: This cover, which was repaired with Peruvian official seals, received air service only within Peru. The cover was posted in Norwich, Connecticut, on November 20, 1928. The official seals were applied on December 4, and a receiving marking on the reverse side indicates the arrival in Lima on December 6.

The cover shown in Figure 13 was posted in Norwich, Connecticut on November 20, 1928. Because this date was prior to the inauguration of air service to Peru, this cover was carried by boat from New York to Talara, Peru. Additionally, it was marked and prepaid for air service within Peru on the route from Talara to Lima, which was announced in the December 1928 *Postal Guide Supplement*. The rate for mail given this service was 25 cents per half ounce, plus the regular postage to Peru of 2 cents per ounce. The cover also bears two Peruvian official seals.

Post cards or postal cards, receiving the service discussed in this article, are quite unusual because the savings relative to sending a letter were very small. A postal card which received air service from London to Berlin is shown in Figure 14 (page 57).

Conclusion

The study of rates and routes of foreign airmail of the 1928 through 1930 period is both quite complex and intriguing. Many fascinating covers remain to be deciphered, and many also remain to be discovered. The serious students of airmail rates and routes can not do without the Post Office Department "bibles" of the time, the annual *Postal Guides* and the monthly *Postal Guide Supplements*. These volumes should be studied in depth as they contain not only vital information on a "problem cover" of the moment, but they also give facts which should be stored away in the mind for future reference.

Bibliography:

Blumenthal, Frank et al. 1981. "Foreign Contract Air Mail Routes. Under designation of the U. S. Post Office Department and U.S. Postal Service, including WIAE and NYRBA service." *American Air Mail Catalogue.* Vol 4 ed 5: 1743-2078. Cinnaminson, New Jersey: American Air Mail Society.

United States Post Office Department. 1932. *Postal Laws and Regulations.* Washington, DC: Government Printing Office

United States Post Office Department. 1929. *United States Official Postal Guide July 1929.* Washington, DC: Government Printing Office.

United States Post Office Department. 1930. *United States Official Postal Guide July 1930.* Washington, DC: Government Printing Office.

United States Post Office Department. 1928, 1929, 1930. *United States Official Postal Guide, Monthly Supplements.* July 1928 through December 1930. Washington, DC: Government Printing Office.

Kent J. Kobersteen studies and exhibits the production and usage of the Beacon airmail stamp of 1928. His exhibit has been awarded national golds. His memberships include the American Air Mail Society, American Philatelic Society, American Association of Philatelic Exhibitors, Bureau Issues Association, Perfins Club, Metropolitan Air Post Society, and the Washington D.C. Philatelic Society.

Table I

United States Foreign Airmail Rates to CENTRAL AMERICA, SOUTH AMERICA and the CARIBBEAN
August 1, 1928 (or inauguration of service) through 1930

Dates given are the first date of rate, or date notice given of a rate change "effective immediately." Rates are per half ounce, or fraction thereof, unless otherwise noted.

Various countries, including Colombia, Ecuador, Peru, Brazil, etc., had private internal airmail carriers which levied a surcharge for mail carried on their routes. Rates for mail carried on these routes are not reflected in this table.

The December 1929 *Postal Guide Supplement* lists numerous rate changes for Central and South America and the Caribbean. In some cases, rates were listed for destinations for which an air service had not yet been inaugurated.

The information in the following tables was extracted from the *United States Postal Guide Supplements* and are quoted in the foot-notes as follows:

a: June 1929 *Postal Guide Supplements*

b: August 1929 *Postal Guide Supplements*

c: September 1929 *Postal Guide Supplements*

d: October 1929 *Postal Guide Supplements*

Table I - 1 — United States Foreign Airmail Rates
to Central America, South America and the Caribbean
August 1, 1928 (or inauguration of service) through 1930

Country	Date and rate at Inauguration		Subsequent rate changes	
Argentina [*4]	Oct 14, 1929	75¢	Jan 1, 1930	55¢
Bahamas	Jan 2, 1929 per half ounce plus 2¢ per ounce	5¢	Mar 20, 1929	5¢
Barbados	Jan 1, 1930	20¢		
Bolivia [*2, 5]	Aug 1929	55¢	Jan 1, 1930	40¢
Brazil	Nov 10, 1930	50¢		
Canal Zone	Feb 4, 1929 per half ounce plus 2¢ per ounce	25¢	Mar 20, 1929 Jan 1, 1930	25¢ 20¢
Chile [*3]	Jul 16, 1929	70¢	Jan 1, 1930	50¢
Colombia [*1]	May 14, 1929	40¢	Jan 1, 1930	30¢
Costa Rica	Jan 1, 1930	20¢		
Cuba	Aug 1, 1928 per half ounce plus 2¢ per ounce	5¢	Mar 20, 1929	5¢
Dominican Republic	Jan 9, 1929 per half ounce plus 2¢ per ounce	10¢	Mar 20, 1929	10¢
Dutch West Indies [*1]: Curacao, Bonaire, Aruba,	Jun 21, 1929 Jun 21, 1929 Jun 21, 1929	40¢ 40¢ 40¢	Jan 1, 1930 Jan 1, 1930 Jan 1, 1930	30¢ 30¢ 30¢

[*1] Service available by sea from the United States to Cristobal, thence by air, at 15 cents per half ounce (a, b, c).

[*2] Service available by sea from the United States to Cristobal, thence by air at 30 cents per half ounce (a, b).

[*3] Service available by sea from United States to Cristobal, thence by air, at 45 cents per half ounce (b).

[*4] Service available by sea from United States to Cristobal, thence by air to Buenos Aires, thence by ordinary means, at 50 cents per half ounce (d).

[*5] By air to Mollendo, Peru, thence by ordinary means to Bolivia (b).

Table I - 2 — United States Foreign Airmail Rates
to Central America, South America, and the Caribbean

Country	Date and rate at Inauguration		Subsequent rate changes	
D.W.I. (cont'd)				
St.Martin,	Jun 21, 1929	40¢	Jan 1, 1930	30¢
St.Eustatius,	Jun 21, 1929	40¢	Jan 1, 1930	30¢
Saba [*1]	Jun 21, 1929	40¢	Jan 1, 1930	30¢
Ecuador [*1]	Jul 16, 1929	40¢	Jan 1, 1930	30¢
Guadeloupe (incl. Desirade, Les Saintes, Marie Galante, Petite Terre, St.Bartholomew, FrenchSt.Martin)	Oct, 1929	25¢	Jan 1, 1930	20¢
Guatemala	Sep 1, 1930	15¢		
Guianas (British, French, Dutch)	Sep 20, 1929	40¢	Jan 1, 1930	30¢
Haiti	Jan 21, 1929 per half ounce plus 2¢ per ounce	10¢	Mar 20, 1929	10¢
Honduras, British	Sep 21, 1929	15¢		
Honduras, Republic of	Sep 21, 1929	15¢		
Jamaica	Dec 2, 1929	10¢		
Leeward Islands:				
Anguilla,	Oct, 1929	25¢	Jan 1, 1930	20¢
Antigua,	Oct, 1929	25¢	Jan 1, 1930	20¢
Barbuda,	Oct, 1929	25¢	Jan 1, 1930	20¢
Dominica,	Oct, 1929	25¢	Jan 1, 1930	20¢
Montserrat,	Oct, 1929	25¢	Jan 1, 1930	20¢
Nevis,	Oct, 1929	25¢	Jan 1, 1930	20¢
Redonda	Oct, 1929	25¢	Jan 1, 1930	20¢

[*1] Service available by sea from the United States to Cristobal, thence by air, at 15 cents per half ounce (a, b, c).

Table I - 3 — United States Foreign Airmail Rates
to Central America, South America and the Caribbean

Country	Date and rate at Inauguration		Subsequent rate changes	
Leeward (cont'd)				
St.Cristopher,	Oct, 1929	25¢	Jan 1, 1930	20¢
St.Kitts,	Oct, 1929	25¢	Jan 1, 1930	20¢
Brit.Virgin Isl.	Oct, 1929	25¢	Jan 1, 1930	10¢
Martinique	Oct, 1929	25¢	Jan 1, 1930	20¢
Mexico	Oct 1, 1928	20¢	Feb, 1929 per first ounce for each additional ounce	5¢ 10¢
Nicaragua	May 21, 1929	25¢	Jan 1, 1930	15¢
Panama	May 22, 1929	25¢	Jan 1, 1930	20¢
Paraguay [*4, 6]	Jan 1, 1930	55¢		
Peru [*2]	May 14, 1929	55¢	Jan 1, 1930	40¢
Puerto Rico	Mar 20, 1929 per half ounce plus 2¢ per ounce	10¢	Mar 20, 1929	10¢
Salvador (El)	Jan 1, 1930	15¢		
Trinidad	Sep 20, 1929	25¢	Jan 1, 1930	20¢
Uruguay [*4, 6]	Jan 1, 1930	55¢		
Venezuela [*1]	Jan 1, 1930	30¢		
Virgin Isl. (US)	Sep 20, 1929	10¢		
Windward Islands:				
Grenada,	Oct, 1929	25¢	Jan 1, 1930	20¢
Grenadines,	Oct, 1929	25¢	Jan 1, 1930	20¢
St.Lucia,	Oct, 1929	25¢	Jan 1, 1930	20¢
St.Vincent	Oct, 1929	25¢	Jan 1, 1930	20¢

[*1] Service available by sea from the United States to Cristobal, thence by air, at 15 cents per half ounce (a, b, c).
[*2] Service available by sea from the United States to Cristobal, thence by air at 30 cents per half ounce (a, b).
[*4] Service available by sea from United States to Cristobal, thence by air to Buenos Aires, thence by ordinary means, at 50 cents per half ounce (d).
[*6] By ordinary means from Buenos Aires at 75 cents per half ounce (d).

Table II - 1

Airmail Routes
LONDON to CONTINENT service
as published in the July 1929 *United States Postal Guide*

1.	London — Paris
2.	London — Paris — Basel — Zurich
3.	London — Paris — Basel — Genoa — Ostia (for Rome) — Naples — Corfu — Athens — Crete — Alexandria — Gaza — Baghdad — Basra — Bushire — Lingeh — Jask — Gwadar — Karachi
5.	Paris — Lyons — Marseilles
12.	London — Ostend — Brussels — Cologne
13.	Cologne — Berlin, etc.
14.	Cologne — Frankfort — Munich, etc.
15.	London — Rotterdam — Amsterdam — Hamburg — Berlin — Vienna
16.	Rotterdam — Essen — Kassel — Prague
17.	Hamburg —Copenhagen — Malmo — Stockholm — Helsingfors — Tallinn (Reval)
18.	Berlin — Königsberg — Kauunas — Moscow
19.	Toulouse — Casablanca — Saint Louis (Senegal) — Dakar

Airmail fees for service on these routes:

Rates are per ounce, or fraction thereof, except where noted, and are in addition to the ordinary postage to the country in question. Except as noted following the airmail fee, the ordinary postage for letters was 5 cents for the first ounce and 3 cents for each additional ounce, or fraction thereof, and 3 cents for post cards.

Table II - 2

Airmail Rates
LONDON to CONTINENT Service
as published in the July 1929 *United States Postal Guide*

from LONDON to:		from LONDON to:	
Africa — North Algeria, Morocco (French Zone), Tangier, Tetuan, Larache, Tunis	8¢	Germany	4¢
		Greece	8¢
[Ordinary postage to Tangier, 2¢ per ounce for letters 1¢ for post cards]		India, per half ounce	12¢
West Africa — French Guinea, Senegal, Gambia, Belgian Congo, Sierra Leone	24¢	India, Aden, Ceylon, Straits Settlements, etc. to overtake the ordinary mail of the previous day	4¢
Austria	6¢	Iraq, Kuwait a) per half ounce, on air route No. 3	9¢
Belgium	4¢	b) per ounce for ordinary route to Gaza, thence by air	6¢
Cyprus	4¢	c) per ounce by air to Marseilles to overtake mail on ordinary route to Gaza	10¢
Czechoslovakia	6¢		
Danzig (Free City)	4¢	Italy	4¢
Denmark	6¢	Latvia	10¢
Egypt and Anglo—Egyptian Sudan a) per half ounce on air route No. 3, which gives delivery to Alexandria from London in four days	5¢	Lithuania	10¢
		Memel	10¢
		Netherlands	4¢
b) per ounce for air routes No. 1 and No. 5, which overtakes preceding mails and gains up to two days	4¢	Norway	6¢
		Palestine, Syria, Transjordan a) per half ounce on air route No. 3	5¢
Estonia (Talinn)	10¢		
Finland	10¢	b) per ounce via Alexandria.	4¢
France	4¢		

Table II - 3

Airmail Rates
LONDON to CONTINENT Service
as published in the July 1929 *United States Postal Guide*

from LONDON to:	from LONDON to:	
Persia	Persian Gulf ports	
a) per half ounce on air	per half ounce	12¢
route No. 3 9¢		
b) per ounce on ordinary route	Russia and Siberia	14¢
to Gaza, thence by air 6¢		
c) per ounce by air to	Sweden	6¢
Marseilles, to overtake mail		
on ordinary route to Gaza 10¢	Switzerland	4¢

Figure 14: For countries where the surface rate for letters was 5 cents, the postcard rate was 3 cents. When the letter rate was 2 cents, the postcard rate was also 2 cents. The Beacon on this postcard paid the 4-cent air rate from London to Germany, plus the additional 1 cent of the 3-cent post card rate to Germany.

Table III - 1

Airmail Routes
PARIS to CONTINENT Service
as published in the July 1929 *United States Postal Guide*

1. Paris — Lyons — Marseilles
2. Marseilles — Ajaccio
3. Toulouse — Perpignan
4. Marseilles — Perpignan
5. Paris — Bordeaux
6. Paris — Strasbourg
7. Marseilles — Algiers
8. Marseilles — Ajaccio — Tunis
9. Toulouse — Perpignan — Barcelona — Alicante — Malaga — Tangier — Rabat — Casablanca
10. Marseilles — Perpignan — Barcelona —Alicante — Malaga— Tangier — Rabat — Casablanca
11. Toulouse — Casablanca — Agadir — Cape Juby — Villa Cisneros — Port Etienne — St. Louis — Dakar
12. Marseilles — Casablanca — Agadir — Cape Juby — Villa Cisneros — Port Etienne — St. Louis — Dakar
15. Paris — London
16. Lyons — Geneva
17. Basel — Geneva — Marseilles — Barcelona
18. Paris — Cologne — Berlin
19. Paris — Berlin (direct)
20. Paris — Saarbrücken — Frankfort (Main) — Berlin
21. Paris — Brussels
22. Paris — Brussels — Rotterdam — Amsterdam
23. Paris — Amsterdam (direct)
24. Paris — Brussels — Rotterdam — Amsterdam — Hamburg — Copenhagen — Malmo
25. Paris — Cologne — Dortmund — Hamburg — Copenhagen — Malmo
26. Paris — Basel
27. Paris — Strasbourg — Nürnberg — Prague — Warsaw
28. Paris — Strasbourg — Nürnberg — Prague — Vienna — Budapest — Belgrade — Bucharest — Stamboul — (Belgrade — Sofia) Stamboul

Table III - 2

Airmail Rates
PARIS to CONTINENT Service
published in the July 1929 *United States Postal Guide*

from PARIS to:		from PARIS to:	
Africa West Coast	24¢	Kingdom of Serbs, Croats and Slovenes	8¢
Algeria	6¢	Morocco	8¢
Austria	6¢	Netherlands	4¢
Belgium	4¢	Poland	6¢
Bulgaria	8¢	Romania	8¢
Czechoslovakia	6¢	Spain [Ordinary postage: 2¢ per ounce for letters, 1¢ for post cards.]	4¢
Denmark	6¢		
France	4¢		
Germany	4¢	Sweden	6¢
Great Britain [Ordinary postage: 2¢ per ounce for letters, 2¢ for post cards.]	4¢	Switzerland	4¢
		Tunis	6¢
Hungary	6¢	Turkey (Europe)	8¢

Airmail fees for service on these routes, per ounce or fraction thereof, and in addition to ordinary postage, is listed above. Except as noted in brackets following the airmail fee, the ordinary postage for letters was 5 cents for the first ounce and 3 cents for each additional ounce, or fraction thereof; and 3 cents for post cards.

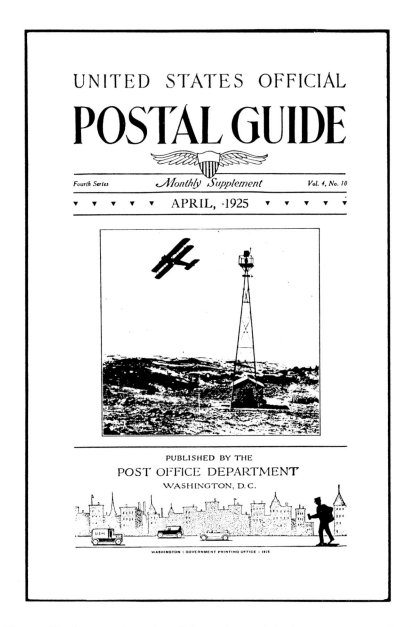

Figure 15: A composite print of three views of the beacon tower received numerous promotional uses before being adapted for the vignette of the "Beacon" stamp.

3

United States

Zeppelin Mail Rates

by Cheryl Ganz

Zeppelin airships were instrumental in establishing air postal routes over long distances, while demonstrating the public's enthusiasm and need for flown mail. They provided the fastest link over oceans and continents for passengers, mail and freight from 1924 to 1937.

Mail franked with United States postage was flown to, from, and within the United States by several airships during this Zeppelin era. in addition to the German *Graf Zeppelin* and *Hindenburg*. United States Navy rigid airships had direct structural relationships to the Zeppelin airship designs and patents, thus qualifying them in this presentation as having flown United States Zeppelin mail. The following rigid airships flew United States mail:

ZR1 *Shenandoah*, built by the United States Navy at Lakehurst, New Jersey, was based on the design of the L49 Zeppelin which was force landed in France in 1917during World War I. The 680 foot long airship flew from September 1923, to September 1925, when it crashed in Ohio.

LZ126 ZR3 *Los Angeles* was built for the United States Navy by the Luftschiffbau Zeppelin in Friedrichshafen, Germany. It was 658 feet and 4 inches long and flew from August 1924 until it was dismantled in 1939.

ZRS4 *Akron* was built by the Goodyear-Zeppelin Corporation in Akron, Ohio. It was 785 feet long and flew from September 1931, until its crash in April 1933.

ZRS5 *Macon* was built by the Goodyear-Zeppelin Corporation in Akron, Ohio. It was 785 feet long and flew from April 1933, until its crash in February 1935.

LZ127 *Graf Zeppelin* was built by the Luftschiffbau Zeppelin in Friedrichshafen. It was 775 feet long and flew from September 1928, until 1937. It was dismantled in 1940.

LZ129 *Hindenburg* was built by the Luftschiffbau Zeppelin in Friedrichshafen. It was 803 feet and 10 inches long and flew from March 1936 until its crash in May 1937.

Both official mail and unofficial mail were flown by Zeppelins. Official mail was authorized by the United States Post Office Department, which handled acceptance and delivery of the mail. If the current surface or airmail rate was inadequate, then special rates were announced.

Unofficial mail was frequently carried by a passenger or a crew member, postmarked before or after the flight at the local post office. Examples of unofficial mail carried at regular surface and airmail postage rates would include all mail flown on the *Shenandoah* and *Macon*, plus a few flights of the *Los Angeles* and *Akron*.

Rates for the flights of rigid airship dispatches from the United States have not been readily available to collectors. An examination of classic references, including *The Dworak Specialized Catalog of U.S. and Canadian Air Mail Covers*, *Handbook of Zeppelin Letters & Postal Cards*, *Handbuch der Luftpostkunde*, the *Sieger Zeppelinpost Spezial-Katalog,* and the *American Air Mail Catalogue* indicate either no rate information or conflicting rate information on some flights. The number of pieces flown also conflicts in these references. This may be due to varying calculations of weight or volume into an estimated number of pieces.

Rates presented here are taken from United States Post Office Department announcements, *The Postal Bulletin,* but also by examination of Zeppelin flown cards and covers. These tables represent not only announced rates and routes, but also changes in service that were unannounced. Arrival and departure dates are taken from log books and listings that correct previously published catalog inaccuracies. Quantities listed in the tables are taken primarily from the *American Air Mail Catalogue*, the *Log Book of the USS Los Angeles* and from an unpublished *Hindenburg* document, found in the Lighter-Than-Air Society Archives.

Figure 1: Posted at the first class 2 cents rate, flown from Lakehurst to Bar Harbor. Mail was placed on board the *Shenandoah* with the aid of the Lakehurst, New Jersey, postmaster, although the mail was carried unofficially.

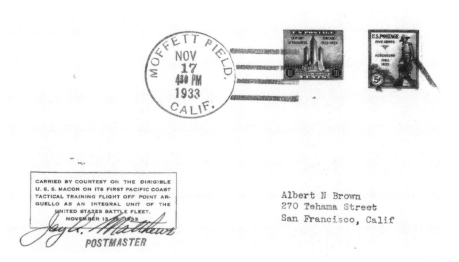

Figure 2: One of 24 souvenir pieces carried by an officer of the *Macon* during a training flight. Posted at the 8 cents airmail rate, although not recognized by postal authorities as official airmail flown by airship.

Table 1: *Los Angeles* **Bermuda and Puerto Rico Flights, 1925**

Route	Date	Card/Letter Rate	Quantity
Lakehurst—Bermuda	Feb 20-21	$0.02	85 lbs (2,341+ pieces)
Lakehurst—Bermuda	Apr 21-22	$0.02	4 bags to *USS Patoka*, 6 bags to Hamilton
Bermuda—Lakehurst dispatched from *USS Patoka*	Apr 23-24	$0.02	95 lbs mostly Bermuda dispatches
Lakehurst— Puerto Rico	May 3-4	$0.02	about 200 lbs
Puerto Rico— Lakehurst	May 8-10	$0.02	5 bags totalling 334 lbs

Note: Letters per ounce, no registered mail.

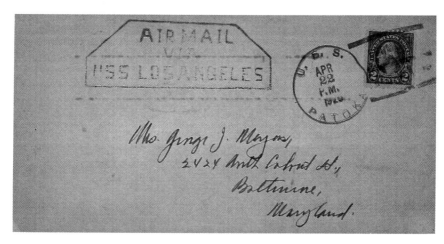

Figure 3: Posted by Captain George J. Meyers of the *USS Patoka*, mooring ship for the *Los Angeles*, and flown from Bermuda to Lakehurst at the 2 cents rate.

Table 2: *Akron* **Transcontinental and Training Flights, 1932**

Route	Date	Card/Letter Rate	Quantity
Lakehurst—San Diego	May 8-11	$0.05	41,705 pieces
Lakehurst—Lakehurst	Aug 1-2	$0.08	65,000 pieces

Note: Rate per ounce, no registered mail.

Figure 4: Carried at regular 8 cents airmail rate by the *Akron*, autographed by crew members Moody E. Erwin and Lieutenant Commander Herbert V. Wiley.

Table 3: *Graf Zeppelin* **America Flight, 1928**

Route	Date	Card Rate	Letter Rate	Quantity
Lakehurst— Friedrichshafen	Oct 29-Nov 1	$0.53	$1.05	101,683 pieces

Note: Rates reflect the Zeppelin fee plus regular foreign mail rate not exceeding one ounce. Special delivery, registration, and United States airmail rate extra.

Figure 5: 50 cents card Zeppelin rate plus regular foreign 3 cents rate per one ounce flown on the first flight to the United States by the *Graf Zeppelin*.

Table 4: *Graf Zeppelin* **World Flight, 1929**

Route	Date	Card Rate	Letter Rate	Quantity
Lakehurst—Friedrichshafen	Aug 7-10	$0.53	$1.05	23,946 pieces
Lakehurst—Tokyo	Aug 7-19	$1.03	$2.05	1,112 pieces
Lakehurst— Los Angeles	Aug 7-26	$1.78	$3.55	300 pieces
Lakehurst— Lakehurst	Aug 7-29	$1.78	$3.55	12,000 pieces
Los Angeles— Lakehurst	Aug 27-29	$0.30	$0.60	10,000 pieces, loaded in Los Angeles
Los Angeles— Friedrichshafen	Aug 27-Sep 4	$0.90	$1.80	10,000 pieces, loaded in Los Angeles
Lakehurst— Friedrichshafen	Sep 1-4	$0.60	$1.20	large quantities (no cachet)

Note: Rates reflect Zeppelin fee plus regular postage; one ounce or less; no registered mail; special delivery and United States airmail rates extra.

Figure 6: The Lakehurst to Los Angeles leg of the World Flight of the *Graf Zeppelin* required $3.50 plus the 5 cents regular rate. This item includes an additional 10 cents for special delivery.

Table 5: *Graf Zeppelin* Pan American Flight, 1930

Route	Date	Card Rate	Letter Rate	Quantity
(United States) Friedrichshafen— Pernambuco	May 18-22	$1.30	$2.60	385 cards, 439 letters
Friedrichshafen— Rio	May 18-25	$1.30	$2.60	
(United States) Friedrichshafen— Seville	May 18-19	$0.65	$1.30	719 pieces
(United States) Friedrichshafen via Brazil—Lakehurst	May 18-31	$1.30	$2.60	19,930 pieces
Lakehurst—Seville	Jun 3-5;			
Lakehurst— Friedrichshafen	Jun 3-6	$0.65	$1.30	2,362 cards, 28,863 letters
(United States) Friedrichshafen— Seville	May 18-Jun 5	$1.95	$3.90	
Friedrichshafen— Friedrichshafen	May 18-Jun 6	$1.95	$3.90	63 cards, 2,168 letters

Note: These rates are not exceeding one ounce. No registered mail. Friedrichshafen—Lakehurst rate includes airmail in the United States.

Figure 7: The complete trip, Friedrichshafen—Friedrichshafen via South and North America required $3.90 on the *Graf Zeppelin's* Pan American flight. Mail was dispatched from New York to reach Germany before the flight began.

Table 6: *Graf Zeppelin* **Chicago Flight, 1933**

Route	Date	Card/Letter Rate	Quantity
(United States) Friedrichshafen— Pernambuco or Rio	Oct 14-17	$0.50	6,743 pieces
(United States) Friedrichshafen— via Brazil— Miami	Oct 14-23	$1.00	2,127 pieces
(United States) Friedrichshafen— via Brazil— Akron	Oct 14-25	$1.50	2,127 pieces
(United States) Friedrichshafen— via Brazil— Chicago	Oct 14-26	$1.00	2,389 pieces
(United States) Friedrichshafen— Seville	Oct 14-31	$2.00	3,407 pieces
(United States) Friedrichshafen— Friedrichshafen	Oct 14-Nov 2	$2.00	3,407 pieces
Miami—Akron	Oct 24-25	$0.50	2,229 pieces
Miami—Chicago	Oct 24-26	$0.50	12,207 pieces
Miami—Seville	Oct 24-31	$1.00	very few
Miami— Friedrichshafen *	Oct 24-Nov 2	$1.00	very few
Akron—Chicago	Oct 26	$0.50	4,285 pieces
Akron—Akron round trip	Oct 26	$0.50	1,993 pieces
Chicago—Akron	Oct 26	$0.50	2,394 pieces
Chicago—Seville	Oct 26-31	$0.50	1,599 pieces
Chicago— Friedrichshafen	Oct 26-Nov 2	$0.50	15,387 pieces
Akron—Seville	Oct 28-31	$0.50	1,218 pieces
Akron— Friedrichshafen	Oct 28-Nov 2	$0.50	8,099 pieces

Note: These rates are per half ounce, no registered mail.
* Rate not announced in advance, but accepted at post offices.

Figure 8: The $1 Miami—Europe rate on the *Graf Zeppelin* Chicago flight was not initially announced by the Post Office Department, although a few pieces were accepted. This cover was sent Miami to Akron, removed from the airship during the Chicago loop, and placed back on board for the Akron to Seville leg.

Figure 9: The first eastbound flight of the *Hindenburg* from Lakehurst to Frankfurt required 40 cents. This cover includes an additional 3 cents for United States airmail and 3 cents for airmail within Europe.

Table 7: *Hindenburg* **Flights, 1936 and 1937**

Lakehurst—Frankfurt	Card/Letter Rate	Quantity
per half ounce *	$0.40	
per half ounce + U.S. airmail	$0.43	
per half ounce + Europe airmail	$0.43	
per half ounce + United States and Europe airmail	$0.46	
per half ounce + air rate to Asia or Africa	$0.40	

1936		
	May 12-14	1,817 lbs
	May 21-23	408 lbs
	Jun 24-26	456 lbs
	Jul 4-6	309 lbs
	Jul 15-17	344 lbs
	Aug 10-11	309 lbs
	Aug 20-22	309 lbs
	Sep 22-24	282 lbs
	Oct 1-3	262 lbs
	Oct 10-12	344 lbs
1937	canceled – mail returned or forwarded	

* First flight of 1936 included return to United States address at no extra charge.

Figure 10: Double weight letter mailed June 20 from Chicago for the third eastbound *Hindenburg* flight of 1936. Rate includes 15 cents registration, 80 cents for double weight, 6 cents for United States airmail at double rate, 6 cents for European airmail at double rate to total $1.07.

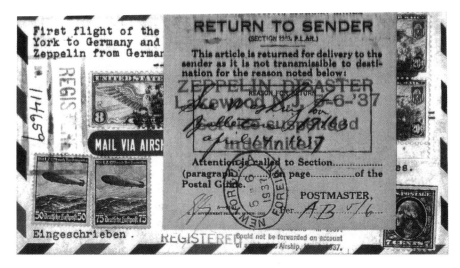

Figure 11: Mail intended for the first eastbound flight of the *Hindenburg* in 1937 was forwarded by regular means or returned to sender. This example received a special 4-line red cachet noting the accident and a return to sender label with a manuscript "See Washington Bulletin 17163 April 14, 1937" referring to *The Postal Bulletin* rates and timetables for 1937 service via the *Hindenburg*.

The earlier *Graf Zeppelin* rates were announced at the ordinary postage rate plus a surcharge rate for the special service. An examination of World Flight covers will quickly demonstrate the confusion this created as many rates are under or over paid. Later inclusive rates were announced for the Pan American and Chicago Flights.

The first mail carried with United States franking, both unofficial and official, was sent at the first class rate on United States Navy airships. As the German Zeppelins sought to fly to and from the United States, they needed the additional revenue from postage in order to help defray the costs of the flight. The higher postage rates for mail carried on various legs was necessary or in some cases the flight route would have been changed.

For example, the extension of the final trip to Brazil of the 1933 season included a flight to the Century of Progress, Chicago World's Fair. The invitation to visit the fair was accepted only if a special stamp would be issued by the United States Post Office Department. The 50-cent stamp showing the Zeppelin, the Federal Building at the Chicago fair and the hangar at Friedrichshafen would mail a half ounce letter. The United States Post Office would receive 15% or 7.5 cents per letter at the 50-cent rate. The remaining 42.5 cents would help to offset the expenses of Luft-schiffbau Zeppelin, as the *Graf Zeppelin* cost $300 an hour to operate, with a crew of forty-seven men. The Zeppelin Company hoped to realize $10,000 from the little green stamp, but actually realized several times that amount. Over 100,000 stamps were flown on souvenir envelopes in addition to mail from many other countries.

On the three previous flights of the *Graf Zeppelin* to the United States, American dispatches accounted for at least half of all postal revenue. According to a report to the Treasury Department of the German Reich on Activities of Luftschiffbau Zeppelin, the company received all money collected by the United States Post Office for mail on these flights.

When the *Hindenburg* began a regular service to the United States from Germany in 1936, the rates were lower than previous *Graf Zeppelin* flights. After the first flight, philatelic cachets were not applied any more and complimentary return service was eliminated. Clearly the Zeppelin Company sought to offer a mail service that was the fastest means across the Atlantic at competitive prices, in addition to service for collectors seeking souvenirs to document the events. Connecting air services and registration were available. In 1937, a 12-cent per ounce Zeppelin fee could be added to regular rates for commercial papers, printed matter, samples of merchandise, printed matter for the blind and small packets.

As the flames of catastrophe burned the *Hindenburg* and most of the on-board mail, they also consumed the hopes of a continued efficient commercial airship service across the Atlantic.

Bibliography

Althoff, William F. 1990. *Sky Ships*. New York: Orion.

Berezowski, Alexander. 1930. *Handbuch der Luftpostkunde, Katalog sämtlicher Marken und Abstempelungen der Luftposten*. Neustadt/Orla: Wagner Verlag.

Berthold, V. M. and F. W. Kummer. 1931. *Handbook of Zeppelin Letters & Postal Cards*. New York: A. Gomez-Sanchez.

Boss, William.O. and Cheryl Ganz. "ZRS4 Akron." *The American Philatelist*. Vol 97 (April 1983.) no 4: 309-320.

Curly, Walter. 1970. *The Graf Zeppelin's Flights to South America*. Weston, Maine: Cardinal Spellman Philatelic Museum.

Dick, Harold G. with Douglas H. Robinson. 1985. *The Golden Age of the Great Passenger Airships Graf Zeppelin & Hindenburg*. Washington, DC: Smith-sonian Institution Press.

Ganz, Cheryl. "The ZR1 Shenandoah." *The American Philatelist*. Vol 102 (November 1988) no 11: 1087-1089.

-----. "The Graf Zeppelin Chicago Flight." *The Airpost Journal*. Vol 57 (May 1986) no 8: 296-299.

-----. "United States Rates for Dispatch on Zeppelin Flights." *The Zeppelin Collector, Air Log & AFA News*. Vol 41 (April 1984) no 2: 57.

Kronstein, Max et al. 1974. "Zeppelin Posts." *American Air Mail Catalogue*. Vol 1 ed 5: 251-306. Washington, DC: American Air Mail Society.

Log Book of the U.S.S. Los Angeles (ZR3). 1925.

Meyer, Henry C. "How Philatelists Kept the Zeppelin Flying." *American Philaelist*. Vol 93 (September 1979) no 9: 796-798.

Nagel, Walter and Max Schnell (Eds). 1931. Section 20—Zeppelins. *The Dworak Specialized Catalog of U.S. and Canadian Air Mail Covers*. Kansas: The Gossip Printery.

The Postal Bulletin. United States Post Office Department. Government Printing Office: Washington, DC. Miscellaneous issues, 1925 through 1937.

Robinson, Douglas H. 1973. *Giants in the Sky*. Seattle, Washington: University of Washington Press.

Sander, Hans. 1989. *Zeppelin Weltrundfahrt 1929*. Germany.

Sieger, Hermann W. 1981. *Sieger Zeppelinpost Spezial-Katalog*. ed 20. Wiesbaden, Germany: Carl Ritter GmbH.

Silver, Philip. 1976. "The $1.00 Rate for Zeppelin Flight, Miami to Friedrichshafen and Seville." *The Aero Philatelist Annals*. Vol 20 no 1: 44-46.

Smith, Richard K. 1965. *The Airships Akron & Macon*. Annapolis, MD: United States Naval Institute.

Tittel, Lutz. 1987. *LZ129 "Hindenburg."* Friedrichshafen. Germany: Städtisches Bodensee Museum.

Additional sources include Post Office Department announcements, the Lighter-Than-Air Society Archives in Akron, the National Archives in Washington, D.C., Dennis Kromm and Henry W. Beecher.

Cheryl Ganz is a collector of zeppelin and balloon mail and related memorabilia. She is currently serving the American Air Mail Society as President and has previously served the Society as Awards Coordinator, on committees and as author, exhibitor and speaker. Cheryl is a Past President of the Chicago Air Mail Society. She has been editor of *The Zeppelin Collector*, newsletter of the Zeppelin Collectors Club from 1977 to present. Other hobby activities include board member of the Chicago Philatelic Society and chair of the literature exhibition of CHICAGOPEX. She chaired the literature committee for AMERIPEX '86. In 1987, she received the Newbury Award for outstanding achievement in Chicagoland philately.

4

World's First Night Airmail,

the 1870 Paris Balloon

Le Général Uhrich

by Ernst M. Cohn

The twenty-ninth manned balloon to be launched during the siege of Paris was *Le Général Uhrich*, named after the general who had been in command of the defense of Strasbourg.

As is true for most balloons of that siege, there was a unique feature about its flight: it was the first of the siege night flights, so it also became the occasion of the world's first night airmail. Another first was use of the world's second airmail cachet, originally in red and then in blue. When was the color changed? The answer is given here — another first.

Background

Several previous day flights had ended in total or partial capture by the enemy. The *Montgolfier's* crew was able to escape on October 25, but the balloon itself and virtually all of the bagged mail were taken. Most of the crew of the privately owned *Bretagne* was captured near Verdun on October 27, its last passenger and the balloon itself a couple of days later. It is doubtful even today whether that balloon carried post office bags.

The *Galilée* was captured shortly after landing on November 4, but part of the mail was saved. The *Daguerre* was shot down on November 12, close to Paris, probably because its sand bags were rotten. This time, one mail bag and a few pigeons were saved from captivity. Paris knew about it two days later.

Something had to be done to protect the balloons, and the answer seemed to be to launch them in the dark. That led to a heated debate, in the Paris newspapers, between two well-known balloonists, then involved in the building of the new siege balloons. Godard appears to have had the stronger influence, meaning that night flights continued. Nadar did not go unheard, however, because the launches were advanced closer toward sunrise, so that the balloons did not have to travel so long during the night.

The only exception was the privately owned *Egalité*, which flew in broad daylight, to prove Wilfrid de Fonvielle's point, viz., that day flight was perfectly safe, provided the pilot (WdF) knew how to fly his balloon properly.

Preparation of the *Général Uhrich*

The departure of the *Général Uhrich* had been announced for "tomorrow 15 November, at mid-night" in a letter from Henri Dommartin, signing for Dartois and Yon, to Dr. Clemenceau, mayor of the 18th district of Paris, later famous French president in World War I. The first night flight was postponed repeatedly, however, because of poor weather.

The balloon's gas bag supposedly consisted of yellow taffeta. Chances are, however, that it only looked yellow to the reporter, be that because of the light or the color of the varnish. It was most likely made of white shirting material, like the other balloons manufactured by Dartois and Yon.

Some hundred people were present for its launching, considered to be a small number by that same reporter.

The pilot of the *Général Uhrich* was a civilian, Emile Martin Lemoine, a mechanic by trade. His passengers were Prosper Thomas, a homing pigeon fancier, and Joseph Bienbar and Jean Chapouil, both members of "Les Francs-Tireurs Sédentaires."

Early sources say that thirty-four or thirty-six homing pigeons were aboard (in contrast to the normal two to ten or twelve), presumably to make up for some thirty pigeons lost with their caretaker Nobécourt in the captured *Daguerre*.

However, pigeon raiser van Roosebeke, also involved in the siege operations, later claimed that the *Général Uhrich* carried only twenty-six pigeons.

Contemporary sources all agreed that the 2000-cubic-meter balloon held 176 pounds of mail. That figure is highly significant (as will be shown later), in contrast to many other contemporary figures cited for weight of mail bags carried by the Paris balloons.

The Flight of the *Général Uhrich*

The balloon, built by "DARTOIS & YON, AÉRONAUTES DU GOUVERNEMENT, RÉPUBLIQUE FRANÇAISE," as their (private) cachet proudly announces, was launched from the North Railway Station on November 18, 1870, at about 11:45 P.M..

As often happens in wartime, the press talked too much and, to correct its impropriety, tried clumsy improvements. Had the Germans really cared, this one would have called special attention to the earlier blunder.

"Due to an error we announced yesterday that the balloon *Le Général Uhrich* had come down near Luzarches. The aeronauts landed much farther away from Paris..."

Apparently a few days later, Pierre Deschamps issued his own denial, concerning the two officers from his personally and privately founded and financed paramilitary unit, the "Francs-Tireurs Sédentaires."

"Sir, I do not know where the *Electeur Libre* got its information, but it announces that 'two free shooters, emissaries of General Trochu,' left for Tours, carried by the balloon *Le Général Uhrich*. Well, at the departure ceremony there were present only some thirty Sedentary Free Shooters, of whom I have the honor to be the captain. They were gathered to say good bye to a very dear friend, delegated by the Government of the Defense, but who was not a member of the corps. Yours, etc. /s/ Pierre Deschamps."

He had neglected only to give the full names of his two lieutenants! So, a few days later the *Electeur Libre* gave two hastily invented names, Bécland and Clapand.

In any case, the *Uhrich* had been in or above the clouds all night long. Wilfrid de Fonvielle claims that its experienced captain, flying above the fog and using different altitudes for changing wind direction as well as using the stars for celestial navigation, managed to stay more or less put near Paris—and that during his very first night flight! A simpler and more convincing explanation, given by Nadar, is that there just was no wind so that the balloon moved very little.

It landed about 8 A.M. some twenty or twenty-five miles from where it had started, near a village named Viarmes, three miles from Luzarches, in the Seine-et-Oise Department. It was necessary to hide everything from the Bavarian unit stationed at Luzarches. The hiding was done with the aid of several Frenchmen. Balloon, basket, anchor, etc. were first stashed away, then moved to a better hiding place in the Abbey of Erivaux, where they still lay in March 1871.

The pigeons had to be moved, of course, and that presented a bigger problem. It was not helped by a circular, published at Tours on November 21 at 4:30 P.M. and sent by the criminal investigation department (!) to all departmental prefects and procurators: " Send to Tours, immediately under escort, a postal employee who landed at Luzarches in the balloon *Général Uhrich*, and who is probably heading for Clermont Ferrand with pigeons. Absolute interdiction of letting him send a single pigeon. All the pigeons must arrive at Tours." Had a copy of that telegram fallen into German hands, they would have had official French information about the landing place and the most important cargo of that balloon. Everything went well, and balloonists as well as pigeons all got to Tours.

The Mail

De Fonvielle claimed that the mail was turned over to the post office at Luzarches. As a matter of fact, all mail personally entrusted to the balloonists, that with the special red PARIS SC postmark, and much of the ordinary mail is marked at Luzarches, 1E/20 NOV 70, i.e., from the first mailbox clearing period of that date.

According to a more thorough researcher, however, some of the mail was taken to the post office of Viarmes, whence the postmistress sent it out during the course of several days, a small package at a time. This fact, although published in the French philatelic press, seems to have been generally ignored.

Assuming that is true, it should be possible to find covers mailed **after** the *Daguerre* had been launched and **before** the *Archimède* had been released, but not postmarked at Luzarches. Such covers should show a **Paris postmark** between 2E/12 NOV and 6E/18 NOV, and earliest **outside** postmarks essentially from before November 21. In fact, early Viarmes mail does exist and is considerably scarcer than Luzarches mail.

Figure 1: The stamp on this folded letter was canceled at Paris with the red PARIS SC postmark used only at the main Post Office. Its earliest outside postmark is from LUZARCHES, 1E/20 NOV 70, which is characteristic for most mail from the *Général Uhrich*.

Figures 1, 2, and 3 show three Viarmes covers I have been able to acquire over the years. Mailed in Paris in mid-afternoon on November 12, November 14, and November 16, they passed through or arrived at France Midi (railway mark), Contres and Tours, all on the 20th, the very day when Luzarches mail was being postmarked there! They are among the not inconsiderable number of sleepers one can still find as part of the siege mails of 1870-71, just by studying closely the sometimes obscure and scattered documentation.

A statistical study first published in France in 1970, later also in the United States, shows that the daily mail load during the siege amounted to perhaps fifty-five to sixty-five pounds, at least after the first few days; on some days it was closer to forty-five pounds.

When it comes to the *Général Uhrich*, mail from almost all of November 12 through almost all of November 18, a total of seven days, was a mere 176 pounds, i.e., half or less than expected for that period. The simplest probable reason is that four people traveled in the car of the balloon, thus limiting its capacity to carry other types of load.

In any case, we have no record whether mail was deliberately held back or taken off the balloon before its launch. The fact remains that, reasoning on purely statistical grounds, roughly half of the mail from that period must have been delayed and taken by the *Archimède* on the 21st. Its mail load more than made up for the difference and apparently not only cleared up the letter mail backlog but it also reduced some of the "second class" mail accumulation.

It must be remembered, therefore, that mail that may have been taken by the *Général Uhrich* should be examined carefully for its **earliest outside postmark**: if the postmark is dated November 20, whether or not from Luzarches, then it is certainly *Uhrich* mail.

If it is later than that date, it may have flown either on that balloon or on the subsequent one, and certain attribution to one of these two balloons may not be possible.

Incidentally, if the cover is water stained and lacks one or more stamps, it may well have flown on the *Archimède*, because a portion of its mail had to be fished out of the sea, something else that most philatelists are unaware of.

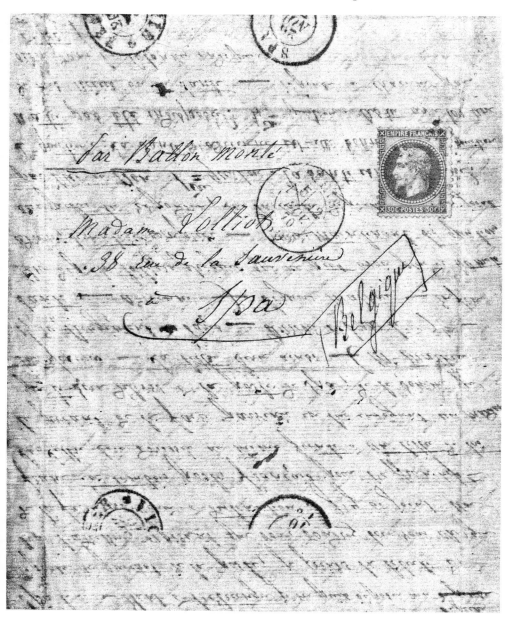

Figure 2: This cover, postmarked 5E/12 NOV (5th clearing period) at the Main Paris Post Office—hence after the departure of the *Daguerre*—has a Belgian transit and an arrival marking at Spa, Belgium, both dated November 20—hence before the departure of the *Archiméde*. It therefore must have flown on the *Général Uhrich*, although not postmarked at Luzarches. Hence this is part of the mail via Viarmes.

The following is taken from information contained in a Paris auction catalogue. The first two lots are from one correspondence, the last eight from another.

Paris postmark	Earliest outside postmark	
Nov 8	France par Tournai	Nov 30
Nov 9	France par Tournai	Nov 30
Nov 12	Spa	Nov 20
Nov 13	Spa	Nov 26
Nov 14	Spa	Nov 23
Nov 15	Spa	Nov 23
Nov 16	Spa	Nov 23
Nov 17	Spa	Nov 23
Nov 19	Spa	Nov 23
Nov 20	Spa	Nov 23

The first two covers were probably sent on the *Daguerre*, in the bag that was saved from capture. Hence the delayed arrival on November 30. The next cover, shown here, is a certain *Uhrich*. That of the 13th is a probably *Uhrich*, mailed too late to be on the *Daguerre*, apparently also in the Viarmes mail but delayed by a few extra days. The mail posted between the 14th and the 17th could certainly have been aboard the *Uhrich*; most likely, however, it was on the *Archimède*, as the last two covers certainly had to be (mailed after the departure of the *Uhrich*). All six covers arrived together at Spa, Belgium, further indirect proof of their having traveled on the same balloon.

On the other hand, if the description of the following lot is correct, then it is certainly a forgery. The newspaper-letter *Le Journal Poste* is supposedly postmarked at Paris on November 13 and at La Guerche on the 17th. Actually, no mail that passed through the Paris post office on the 13th and was destined for the outside could have left Paris before almost the end of the 18th. On the other hand, it is possible that the describer of the lot (or the printer) made a mistake, and that the mail got to La Guerche (Cher, in the Ille-et-Villaine or Indre-et-Loire Department?) on, say, the 27th.

A report in a Belgian paper complains about the delayed distribution of the *Général Uhrich's* mail: "

..An attaché of the (Belgian) embassy (at Tours) told me this morning (November 22) that the (French) government is opposed to delivering the private mail (of the *Général Uhrich*). The interior ministry claims only government mail was carried. The *Moniteur*, official and semi-official newspaper, affirms the contrary. Why does the government make such a mystery about Paris mail..."

Figure 3: The date stamp of 5E/14 NOV of the Paris office at the Rue Cardinal Lemoine cancels the postage stamp, as was normal for this office, which seems to have used its pointed star with the "28" numeral only exceptionally.

Contres arrival mark was struck twice on November 20.

It never occurred to that reporter, writing from Tours on November 22, that the government might be worried about the safety of the *Uhrich's* balloonists and cargo, just as some philatelists today find it difficult to comprehend delays and detours caused by war.

The Aeronauts' Cachet

Of the two builders of wartime balloons, one team sported a private hand stamp:

"REPUBLIQUE-FRANÇAISE/ 1 Aerostiers / Nadar-Dartois Duruof."

When these men, who had wanted originally to observe the enemy from a tethered balloon, decided to build and launch manned mail balloons, someone got the idea of applying the cachet to airmail that was entrusted to their personal care.

The cachet was always stamped in red and only on mail handed to a pilot associated with these "First Aerostiers." The first pilot to fly a mail balloon out of Paris was Duruof, who had sold his *Neptune* to the post office.

The mail bags he had along, however, apparently contained merely delayed printed matter and other second class material, so that the only letters he carried were those entrusted to him personally, some of which bear that Aérostiers' world's first airmail cachet.

To make up for Duruof's absence, Nadar and Dartois persuaded Yon, another experienced aeronaut, to join them. They continued to use the old handstamp, however, until Nadar left the company on October 27, in protest against the government's balloon building policy.

Interestingly, a number of strikes with the Aérostiers handstamp are extant from the *Colonel Charras*, which left around noon on October 29, i.e., after Nadar had quit the Aérostiers. Yet no strikes of either cachet are known from the balloons *Ferdinand Flocon* and *Ville de Châteaudun* though they are theoretically possible. Was the Aérostiers handstamp not usable any more and was the Aéronautes handstamp not yet available during that period?

Anyhow, the latter handstamp was made during that time. It is normally struck in greenish blue, except for a few covers from the *Général Uhrich*, on which it is struck in red. There is no explanation as to why some of the imprints are red, apparently before the stamp pad was changed to blue. One thinks of a rather disturbing possibility:

Both of the rubber handstamps, which are today kept at the Musée de la Poste in Paris, got there via Maury, Tissandier, and Maincent, the last having donated them to the Musée.

It is not known how they came into his possession. He was one of the foremost stamp dealers of the world, a prolific writer, collector, and also creator of a number of falsifications and souvenirs (not to call them fakes) of a postal history nature, relating to the 1870/71 war.

The Aérostiers handstamp had the name of Nadar and the hyphen chopped out of it, at an unknown time. Conceivably, Nadar insisted upon that soon after leaving. The result not only looked bad but also did not take into consideration the fact that Yon was a full partner. There may have been no way to put **his** name on the old stamp; perhaps it was cheaper and simpler to have a new one made. The Aéronautes handstamp is still in its original condition, however.

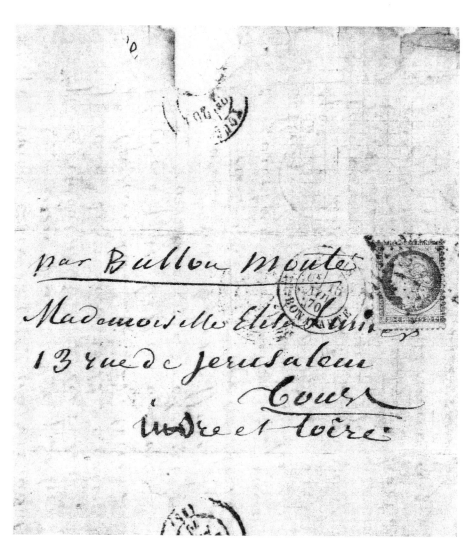

Figure 4: Posted at 6E/16 14NOV at the Post Office on Rue Bonaparte at Paris, the letter arrived at Tours on November 20.

Did Maury "try it out" in red on a few covers? Not likely. We have contrary evidence from a brief survey of the available material, presented in the little tabulation below, which lists six dated Aéronautes cachets in order:

#	R/B	Date	Remarks
1	R	5	discovered by Brun in 1985?, letter from Cappart
2	R	7	*Gazette* #5, Robineau, sale 102, lot 470 (1971)
3	R	15	*Gaulois*, Robineau, C(ourtois) sale, lot 125 (1979)
4	B	15	Robineau, Antonini sale, lot 439 (1974)
5	B	15	LePileur (both editions); also Robineau, C(ourtois) sale, lot 124
6	B	17	*Gazette* #8, Cérès sale, lot 875 (May 1986)

Note: *Gazette* 5 is dated November 5, *Gazette* 8 is dated the 16th. The date for item 3 is apparently the imprint on that issue of the *Gaulois*, which was dated one day ahead.

On the assumption that the cachet was applied when a letter was handed in, this little compilation shows that the cachet was used as early as November 6 (it had to be **after** the departure of the *Ville de Château-dun*!), struck in red until November 14 or 15, and in blue from the 15th onward.

The majority of the Aéronautes strikes on *plis confiés* (personally entrusted covers) of the *Général Uhrich* and all strikes on mail from subsequent balloons are blue. Those in black and strikes on covers postmarked inside Paris have been applied after the siege. They are clearly forgeries.

Conclusion

In gathering together contemporary as well as later evidence about the world's first night airmail, flown on the manned Paris balloon *Le Général Uhrich*, one notices some interesting facts, apparently long ignored.

An effort has been made to check one of these, having to do with mail disposition after landing. That resulted in the discovery of proof, in the form of covers **not** postmarked at Luzarches on November 20, 1870. Hence part of the mail was, in fact, routed not via Luzarches but apparently via Viarmes. There it was not postmarked, but some of it was dispatched thence quicker than from Luzarches. Such covers have to be rare, not just because only a small portion of the Viarmes mail was postmarked very early but also because later Viarmes mail overlaps with mail from the *Archimède* and hence cannot normally be characterized with certainty as to a single balloon.

Another fact is that *Uhrich* mail amounts to perhaps half or less of the total mail that had been accumulated after the previous balloon had been launched. Therefore, the only covers certain to have been aboard are those postmarked at Luzarches and elsewhere on November 20, 1870. (If any exist postmarked on November 19 – and perhaps on November 21 that could not possibly have been aboard the *Archimède* – they have not yet turned up.)

An analysis, made of covers listed in auction catalogues, illustrates some of the factors involved in checking on the authenticity of covers as well as their attribution to a certain balloon.

As for mail personally entrusted to the pilot and hand stamped by one of the balloon builders, it is the first to carry the Aéronautes cachet. It is also the only one that, besides the usual blue strike, contains some covers with a red strike. As has now been determined, the red strikes were made until the November 14 or 15, when a blue ink pad was substituted and used until the end of the siege.

Hence even some of the oldest and presumably best explored instances of airmail carriage still offer opportunities for research that may well result not just in deeper insight into the facts but also in the recognition of rarities that had been overlooked for decades.

Bibliography:

La Belgique, November 26, 1870: 3, Brussels, Belgium.

Letter from H. Cappart to author, April 18, 1970.

Chaintrier, Louis. "A Histoire documentaire et anecdotique des Ballons-Poste du Siège de Paris (1870-71)." *L'Echangiste Universel* (1954-63). The *Général Uhrich* is covered in no 690 (November 1957) and no 692 (January 1958).

Cohn, Ernst M. "The Manned Balloons of the Siege of Paris, A Historical Statistical Approach." *The Airpost Journal*. Vol 43 (April 1972) no 7: 216-219, no 9 (June 1972): 284-87 also front cover, no 12 (September 1972): 396-399.

----- "Les Ballons Montés du Siège de Paris, Essai d'après les statistiques historiques," *L'Aéronaute*. March 1874. *Bulletin* of the Société des Amis du Musée Postal (*Bull. SAMP*) 30, 1970 Vol 7 no 3: 78.

----- "Les départs nocturnes des ballons poste en 1870-71." *Bull. SAMP*. (1968) no 23: 12-18. This paper contains the verbatim copies of all letters to the editor by Nadar and Godard about that subject.

Journal des Débats, November 28, 1870: 3, col 1, quoting *L'Avenir National* which, in turn, copied from *L'Electeur Libre*.

L'Electeur Libre. November 16. 1870: 1.

L'Electeur Libre, November 26, 1870: 1 col 4. It may be noted that this group was authorized by the French war ministry on September 9, 1870 and consisted of 30 to 60-year-olds, commanded by their organizer, Pierre Deschamps. As of October 26 the unit contained 30 men, employed primarily for service within the internal Paris sectors (anon., *La Guerre de 1870-1871*, published by Revue d'Histoire, edited by Section Historique de l'Etat-Major de l'Armée: Vol. 36: 376, *L'Investissement de Paris*, 1908). Starting with the *Uhrich*, however, several volunteers from that group, including Pierre Deschamps himself, flew to the Government Delegation and attempted to return to Paris through the lines, with information. None was successful.

de Fonvielle, Wilfrid. "La chute d'un ballon à Luzarches en 1870." *Mémoires de la Société Historique et Archéologique de Pontoise et du Vexin*, Vol 18: 101-109 (1896), also reprint.

Le Gaulois as quoted in *Le Moniteur Universel*, November 20, 1870: 1558 col 3-4; also in Joseph-François-Frédéric Steenackers, *Les Télégraphes et les Postes pendant la Guerre de 1870-1871*. (1883): 415-16.

Haberer, Rainer. Filderstadt, Germany. 15th airmail auction, lot no 775.

de Limay, Alexis Ratouis. "Extraits du Journal du Siège de Paris (1870-71)." *L'Echo* no 1402 (October 1970): 28-29.

Maincent, Paul. "27 – Le Daguerre," *Icare* (1971) no 56: 119-120.

-----"Histoire de La Bretagne. Aérostat due Siége." *L'Echo de la Timbrologie (L'Echo)* no 1329 (September 1964) through no 1354 (October 1966).

Letter cited by Paul Maincent in "À propos d'une lettre de Clemenceau à sa femme," *L'Echo*, no 1287 (March 1961): 143-144; weather news in *New York Times*, December 12, 1870: 5 col 4.

Mengin, Charles. 1871. *Histoire de la deuxième Armée de la Loire*. Vol 1: 63-69. This is the verbatim report of Colonel Joseph-Marie LeBouëdec (1829-1899), a *Montgolfier* passenger.

Moniteur Universel (Tours), November 24, 1870: 260 refers to issue no 256 of the 23rd..

Roumet S.A., Paris, 381st sale, May 27, 1986, lots no 1962 through 74, exc. 1967 (arrival illegible) and 1970-71 (identical dates to lot 1969).

Ernst Cohn started collecting the siege (air)mails of the 1870/71 Franco-German War. The findings, exhibited and published in several countries, resulted in major catalog revisions and earned him the Aero Philatelists Trophy at SEPAD'67, the Gerard Gilbert Award of the F&CPS in 1978, the FISA Aerophilatelic Literature Award (1981), the FIP medal (Hafnia'87) for research, and many exhibition awards. He was written for the AAMC, helped in the publication of AAMS books, served on AAMS literature award committees, judged exhibits and advised exhibitors. He rendered many (unpaid) reasoned opinions on 1870 covers, some of which he unmasked as forgeries.

5

The 1911

Chicago Air Meet

by Stephen Neulander

"Those magnificent men and their flying machines" came to Chicago for the world's most extravagant air show of its time. The show was a nine-day event, with a total prize purse of $80,000. It was held at Grant Park — in the center of the city of Chicago, adjacent to the city's central business district. Never before or since has an aviation meet of that magnitude been held in the downtown area of one of the world's major cities.

August 12 through 20, 1911, saw almost everyone who was someone in aviation trying for a share of the money, with crowds as big as the population of many smaller cities in attendance for the nine days of flying activities.

This is not a story of airmail, but it is important to the development of airmail service. For without the farsightedness of a small group of Chicago businessmen who were determined to create a hub of aviation activity, the city may not have been ready to accept aviators and airplanes. Yet a fast-growing nation needed a central hub, and the success of the Aero Club of Illinois with its International Aviation Meet of 1911 enabled the United States to have one. In less than ten years, Chicago would become the center of airmail routes from coast to coast.

In 1911, the airplane was considered by most Chicagoans as nothing but a toy! It was for the dreamer and the elite. It was an amusement for the rich and the daredevil. Still there were a handful of men who saw the future with airplanes as an important part of it. The leader of this group was Harold F. McCormick, heir to the McCormick farm tool fortune. For a short period of time, he stopped his globe trotting and indulged his energies in Chicago. There is little doubt that without McCormick's desire for the success of aviation and the Aerial Meet of 1911, the event would not have taken place.

It all started simply enough. Newspaper publishers throughout the world were offering huge sums of money for pilots to fly from here to there, one way or round trip. William Randolph Hearst made an offer of $50,000 to the first man to fly coast to coast. The *New York World* and the *St. Louis Post-Dispatch* would reward with $30,000 anyone who could fly between the two cities. The *World* gave Glenn Curtiss $10,000 for flying from Albany to New York City. And J.C. Shaffer, publisher of the *Chicago Evening Post*, put up $1,000 to go to the first man to fly from Chicago to New York City (or the other way). The competition, the *Chicago Record Herald*, not to be outdone, offered $10,000 for a flight between Chicago and Springfield. So the *Chicago Evening Post* raised its offer to $25,000.

While a great deal of this competition was nothing but publicity for the newspapers making the offers, the Aero Club of Illinois, which had been formed in February 1910, sensed a certain feeling in the excitement that was being created by these newspaper promotions. Taking advantage of that public interest and excitement, the Aero Club influenced the development of general aviation in Chicago for the next two decades, thereby establishing Chicago and its environs as a major capital of aviation for all time.

After the Aero Club was formed, the question arose: "what shall we do to promote aviation in Chicago?" To follow through on ideas presented by the membership, McCormick and Charles Dickinson went to the Belmont Park Air Show in New York in 1910. There they became convinced that the best way to generate interest in aviation in Chicago would be to put on a spectacular Air Meet.

And so the idea was born to stage the 1911 Chicago Air Meet. But implementing the idea was not easy. McCormick proposed the idea to the Club on March 6, 1911. In true Chicago fashion, "do it in a hurry and do not waste time." The directors agreed to hold the Meet, and then sought a suitable field, deciding on Grant Park.

Now all that was left to be done was to raise money, invite the pilots, build the facilities, publicize the event, etc.

Greatest Event in the History of Aeronautics!!

International
Aviation Meet

GRANT PARK

CHICAGO

AUGUST 12-20, 1911

UNDER AUSPICES INTERNATIONAL AVIATION MEET ASSOCIATION
FULL OFFICIAL SANCTION

$80,000 IN PRIZES!

LARGEST PURSE AND MOST AMBITIOUS PROGRAM EVER OFFERED
IN ANY COUNTRY

AVIATION FIELD EXCEEDING ONE MILE IN LENGTH—OVAL COURSE
OVER ONE AND ONE-THIRD MILES IN CIRCUMFERENCE MINIMUM DIS-
TANCE—EVENTS EMBRACE EVERY FEATURE AND NOVELTY IN AVIA-
TION—HANGARS FOR 40 MACHINES—GRAND STAND FOR 50,000 PEOPLE

SPECIAL RAILROAD RATES

NINE DAYS—EVERY AFTERNOON

MANY FREE SEATS

SCALE OF PRICES, 25c. TO $1.50—BOX SEATS $2.00

Figure 1: Contemporary advertisement of the upcoming 1911 Chicago Air Meet (source unknown).

The Aero Club of Illinois had a fund raiser in April 1911, inviting all prominent business and political figures. The Aero Club of America sent Augustus Post to show slides of the Belmont show in 1910.

Figure 2: Orange vignette, promoting the 1911 Chicago Air Meet.

But in the end, McCormick became the show's principal underwriter. He advanced the club $45,000 in cash and he put up a personal bond for $80,000 in prize money.

The Wright Brothers were not keen on the Meet. They wanted to cash in on their patents. Thus they threatened the Meet with lawsuits, and demanded a $10,000 fee to license the Meet. Selfish to the end, they stated that if they had the money they would sue every pilot who entered. "He (Orville Wright) very openly stated there were three things he wanted: first, to prevent foreign aviators from coming to America; second, to get as much money out of the meet as possible; third, to support his patents. He stated that our Meet was a detriment to them rather than a gain. He stated that he did not care whether aviation in America was helped or not," wrote McCormick in his report to the Aero Club after meeting with the Wrights in Dayton.

The Aero Club members decided to proceed with or without the Wright's endorsements. It petitioned the Aero Club of America for official sanction, and received this on July 28, 1911.

In the meantime, the Aero Club made another decision, one unlike any other that had been made for previous meets. It would pay famous names to participate. After all, without these famous flyers the public would not care about the event.

However, the Club would not meet the exorbitant fees being requested. For example, T.O.M. Sopwith of England asked for an advance guarantee of $5,000. The promoters thought that the large purse should be enough incentive for the pilots. It was also the promoters belief that if they underwrote each pilot for as much as the pilot thought he was worth, the pilots would have very little reason to fly.

Figure 3: Getting ready for the International Aviation Week in downtown Chicago (Jim Adams collection).

And the promoters were right. The $80,000 lured the best aviators in the world to Chicago when the pilots were guaranteed that their expenses for getting to Chicago would be covered. In most cases expenses ranged between $250 and $500.

T.O.M. Sopwith, Earle Ovington, J.A.D. McCurdy from Canada, Charles Willard, Réné Barrier from France, Abraham Raygordsky from Russia, and native Chicagoan St. Croix Johnstone all applied for entry. In the end, even the Wrights sent a team.

From April to August everyone was busy planning, building, promoting, and organizing for the Meet. The United States Government sent troops from Fort Rily, Kansas, Fort Sheridan, Illinois, and the Coast Guard Station in Milwaukee, Wisconsin. In the end, the business community and the newspapers finally got into the act, and everything was ready for the big event.

On Saturday, August 12, 1911, thirty-five aviators stood ready to participate in tests of their flying ability. When the cannon sounded for the first event of the day, several hundred thousand people crowded the area near

Grant Park to get a look at "those flying machines." While seats were available for about 63,000 spectators for 50 cents to $2 each, most of the onlookers paid nothing and enjoyed the view from a distance. The Congress Hotel, directly across from the park, advertised that it had rooms offering more than 2,000 windows with a view of what was going on at the Meet.

And what a grand and exciting day it was, with many unscheduled thrills. Starting at 3:00 P.M., the first test of skill was a flight duration contest, followed by an over-water race twice around a three-and-one-half-mile course at 4:30 P.M.. Then at 5:30 P.M., the biplane passenger-carrying race took place, followed by altitude competition at 6:00 P.M., and then a cross-country flying event at 7:00 P.M..

Unscheduled excitement occurred when Arthur Stone, while making a steep turn at low altitude in his Queen Blériot monoplane, forced his wing tip into the ground, flipping the plane on to its back. Then Frank Coffyn crashed his flying machine into a parked Moisant monoplane while making a forced landing with two passengers. René Simon's Moisant left without him on board (as he cranked the prop, it began to run) and crashed into a tree. James Martin in a Bristol-Farman overshot the runway and crashed into a fence. All pilots and passengers escaped injury.

Opening day winners included Earle Ovington who beat T.O.M. Sopwith in the speed races by flying 20 miles in 23 minutes, 52 seconds. C.P. Rogers won the flight duration contest by staying aloft for 2 hours, 55 minutes, 33 seconds. Howard Gill was the winner of the altitude climb. Flying a Wright biplane, Gill reached 4,980 feet to beat Lincoln Beachey, who climbed to 3,507 feet and Phillip Parmelee at 3,273 feet.

Sunday, August 13, dawned brightly. The crowds of the day before had surprised the organizers; today even more people came. An estimated 400,000 spectators showed up, having heard of this event either through word of mouth or newspaper stories. The crowd was so large that some observers could not get closer to the park than State Street.

Those spectators who were close enough to see what was happening were not to be disappointed by the events. A potentially serious accident was avoided by J.J. Frisbie. His plane brushed a statue that topped the 250 foot high Montgomery Ward Building when a sudden gust of wind struck the plane. Because of an injured hand, Frisbie temporarily lost control of his plane, which began a steep downward spiral. Only at the last minute was he able to pull the plane out of its spin and land safely. Beachey continued to thrill the crowd with low spins and dives and turns made at altitudes so low that his tires often touched the ground.

Figure 4: Arthur Stone taking off in his Queen Blériot monoplane (Jim Adams collection).

Figure 5: Curtiss Hydro-aeroplane (A-1), flown by Hugh A. Robinson.

A real showman, Beachey took advantage of the Michigan Avenue congestion to fly across the tops of parked cars, almost touching the roofs as he flew down the Avenue.

The newspapers ate up the excitement and reported events in great detail. This helped to turn out an unusually large crowd of more than 50,000 on Monday, August 14. The spectators were not disappointed. The day's activities included the arrival of Boston aviator Harry Atwood, who was in the process of trying to win a $10,000 prize for being the first to fly from St. Louis to the city of New York. Atwood left St. Louis early in the morning, made stops for fuel in Springfield and Pontiac, and arrived in Chicago after 6 hours, 12 minutes flying time. He left Chicago (Grant Park) the next day and arrived in New York on August 25.

But the real excitement was the accidents which continued to occur although there were no fatalities. First, Réné Simon skidded his Moisant over the waters of Lake Michigan when the engine failed and he glided to a crash landing in the lake. He was rescued by a nearby boat.

Then Lee Hammond's Baldwin biplane snapped a support wire while rounding a crib three and a half miles out into the lake. The loose wire wound itself around the propeller making further flying impossible. Hammond managed to jump to safety just before the plane crashed into the lake. He, too, was rescued by a boat posted nearby.

Earle Ovington's Curtiss plane lost a cylinder while doing pylon turns. His wing hit the ground causing the plane to crash. But Ovington stepped from the wreckage without injury and returned to fly a few moments later in a spare Blériot.

Howard Gill attempted to reach a new altitude record. At 800 feet, the chain drive on his prop broke and he was forced to glide to the ground.

The wing tip of J.A.D. McCurdy's biplane struck a high tension wire while he was attempting a short landing approach. He crashed on the beach and flipped over; he was thrown free.

Unfortunately the good fortune of the first three days did not continue. Tuesday, August 15, saw the death of two aviators. William Badger of Pittsburgh, age 27, died when he attempted a steep dive and waited too long to pull out. From newspaper reports based on spectator eyewitnesses, "he was but 20 feet from the ground." Later that day, St. Croix Johnstone, age 26, was killed when his plane exploded at 1,600 feet and crashed into Lake Michigan. The surviving pilots flew an extra day, August 21, after the official end of the Meet to raise money for Johnstone's widow (Figure 6).

Sᴛ. Cʀᴏɪx ᴊᴏʜɴsᴛᴏɴᴇ.

Figure 6: St. Croix Johnstone in his monoplane which, during the Air Meet, exploded and crashed into Lake Michigan, killing the pilot

Poster of unknown origin promoting an extra day of flying activities to raise money for the widow of St. Croix Johnstone.

(Jim Adams collection)

MONDAY, AUGUST 21
GRANT PARK-LAKE FRONT

Great Testimonial Exhibition
WORLD FAMED AVIATORS

Total Receipts for Benefit of Mrs. St. Croix Johnstone

ALL THE WONDERFUL BIRDMEN VOLUNTEERING A SPLENDID PROGRAM

OPENING SALUTE 4 P. M.

Meet opening at the firing of the bomb at 4.00 p.m. Exhibition speed monoplane flights from 4.00 p.m. to 5.00 p.m. Exhibition speed biplane flights from 5.00 p.m. to 5.30 p.m. A general exhibition by all the aviators with their aeroplanes showing the control of the aeroplane in landing and starting, etc., also many unexpected flights and tricks by the aviators, which up until the present time they have been unable to do, between the hours of 5.30 p.m. and 6.30 p.m. or the firing of the last bomb.

Prices, 50c to $1.50; Box Seats 32.00

Tickets on sale at Auditorium Theater Box Office, principal State street Stores and Downtown Hotels. Contribution Depositories at Free Grand Stand.

Chicago Historical Society

Broadside announcing a benefit program for the widow of St. Croix Johnstone, who was killed when his plane crashed into Lake Michigan on Aug. 15.

After the fatalities, there were outcries to stop the Meet. However, the aviation authorities decided to continue. They believed that there was much to be learned about flying, and that a continuation would increase knowledge that might lead to the ending of tragic air accidents.

While there were no further fatal accidents, there were still many mishaps to occur. The major problem was the winds which swept over the hot city during August. The citizen's best friend, off-lake-winds, was the enemy of the pilots. In fact, Orville Wright instructed those pilots flying Wright aeroplanes to resist taking their planes up in certain wind conditions. But the rewards for flying were too great and tempting. Beachey and Eugene Ely both flew against these directions by the Wright Company. Other winds were also troublesome. Strong winds from the west were often blocked by the tall buildings to the west of Grant Park. Due to these swirly winds, take-offs into the wind were dangerous and tricky.

The remainder of the week saw some strange events. The "bombing of ships," a mock battle, was but one. There were also many attempts at new records, but these were not to be accomplished until the last day of the Meet.

On Friday, the seventh day, Oscar Brindley attempted to set a new altitude record. He wanted to best Beachey's 8,500 feet, Parmelee's 10,837 feet, but also the French record of 11,152 feet. Brindley was unsuccessful.

Beachey was not denied the honor of a new world's altitude record. On the last official day of the Meet, Saturday, Beachey used every drop of gas in his custom Curtiss built plane; using his entire supply of fuel, he climbed to 11,578 feet, and then glided safely back to the ground in majestic splendor. This record was to stand for three years. It had taken Beachey over 1 hour and 45 minutes to reach the new altitude record, but it took only 12 minutes to glide back to Grant Park.

Two other international records were set. T.O.M. Sopwith and Réné Simon tied for one, each climbing 1,634 feet in 3 minutes, 25 seconds. Both men flew Blériot planes. The other record, set by the Wright team, was for a duration flight. C.A. Beatty set the record by carrying a passenger in his biplane for 3 hours, 38 minutes.

The 1911 International Aviation Meet in Chicago was probably the most extravagant and most publicized of all Air Meets staged in the United States prior to September 1911 when the first "Pioneer Airplane Mail" was flown as part of the Garden City Estates Meet on Long Island, New York. These early aviation events frequently produced items which are eagerly collected and which are historically as well as aerophilatelically significant.

Figure 7: William R. Badger in his Baldwin biplane. Card was posted on August 22, 1911, showing the time-marking machine cancel from the Main Chicago Station. The letter "C" indicates the item was brought to the Main Post Office to be placed in the mail.

Aviation and other souvenir photo cards, labels and posters were readily available for purchase. Shown in this article are aviation postcards from the 1911 Chicago Air Meet, some where posted at different postal substations in the city. Some of these cards may have been flown by a pilot and handed back after the flight, but none of these cards were carried as "official mail," although they were forwarded through the Post Office Department mail system. They are not considered to be "Pioneers."

What should be of interest to collectors of early aviation material is the fact that although no signed and flown cards have yet been found, it is more than possible that such souvenirs do exist and patience will bring them out. In the early years of the century, every corner of Michigan Avenue paralleling Grant Park had a postal box for outgoing mail. The hotels on the west side of the street also had postal pick-up and delivery service; thus the possibility of a card being flown and quickly posted does exist. At this time there was no governmental interest and although it had been contacted to participate in ways other than supplying necessary troops, the thought of "airmail" and use of the aeroplane as a form of communication was almost unheard of.

The following year, 1912, official pioneer airmail was flown as part of the Cicero Air Meet (September 12 through 14), but also at Grant Park (September 16 through 22).

Looking back, what was accomplished by the event? Although the Chicago Aviation Meet of 1911 was hailed in the city and throughout the aviation world as a huge success, it was a financial failure. The organization took in $145,635 in revenue from tickets, programs, and advertising, but it lost $56,121. And because of the lawsuit still pending by the Wright Brothers, the International Aviation Meet Association was forced to assess its members a total of $75,000. In addition to paying out more than $102,938 in prize money to participating aviators, expenses like preparing Grant Park for the Meet, construction of grandstands and hangars, bands and entertainment for the crowds, administrative expenses, field hospitals, and advertising and publicity totalled $98,818. The grand total of all expenditures was $201,756.

There was plenty of nitpicking done by committee members. One of the founding members, Victor Lougheed, resigned from the Aero Club charging graft, corruption, and mismanagement of the Air Meet. The Board protested, stating were it not for McCormick there would not have been a show at all.

By that time, though, nothing mattered anymore. McCormick and the Aero Club of Illinois were looking at new projects, one of which was the development of Chicago's first real airport, Cicero Field.

Figure 8: Flying activities during the 1911 Chicago Air Meet.

By the end of 1912, general aviation in Chicago was on a sound and growing footing. An irreversible momentum had been established. Would-be aviators from around the country and the world came to Cicero Field to train at one of the nation's best flying schools.

In 1918, the United States Post Office Department's long-range plan called for a transcontinental air route from New York to San Francisco. Naturally, the center of the transcontinental airmail route was Chicago. And Chicago today still is the hub for many feeder lines.

Bibliography:

Bushnell, George D. "The International Aviation Meet, 1911." *Chicago History.* Spring 1976. Chicago, Illinois: Chicago Historical Society.
Karlen, Dr. Harvey M. 1971. *Chicago Postal History.* Chicago, Illinois: Collectors Club of Chicago. Also discussion with and comments from the author.
Scamehorn, Howard L. 1957. *Balloons to Jets, 1855-1955, A Century of Aeronautics in Illinois.* Illinois State Historical Society Occasional Publications. No 52. Chicago, Illinois: Henry Regnery Comp.

Young, David and Neal Callahan. 1981. *Fill the Heavens with Commerce, Chicago Aviation, 1855-1926*. Chicago, Illinois: Chicago Review Press.

Aeronautics Magazine. Miscellaneous issues, August and September 1911.

The Chicago Tribune, August 7 through 22, 1911.

The Chicago Daily News, August 7 through 22, 1911.

The Chicago Inter Ocean, August 7 through 22, 1911.

Aero Club of Illinois files, courtesy of Chicago Historical Society, Chicago, Illinois.

CAMS, *Chicago Air Mail Society Bulletin*. Miscellaneous issues, 1982 through today.

Interview with Sydney Wolfson, United States Postal Service, Chicago (Ret'd).

Stephen Neulander is the president of the Jack Knight Air Mail Society and the Balloon Post Specialists and edits the newsletter of the CAMS, *Chicago Air Mail Society Bulletin*. He is active in aerophilately from a historical point of view since becoming the first hot air balloon pilot to cross Lake Michigan in 1975. He is a past president of the Chicago Air Mail Society, was the promotion director for AMERIPEX '86. Steve is chairman of *Aerophilately 1992*, is active in COMPEX and CHICAGOPEX and received the Ben Reeves award for literature from COMPEX. His collecting interests include Blériot, Women in Aviation, Chicago & Southern Airways and several balloon related subjects.

6

Early Chicago Area

Airports

and

Airmail Dedications

by **Raymond Broms**

Throughout the United States there have been many first flights since the establishment of the official routes in 1918. Most of these flights were executed with great enthusiasm. Dignitaries as well as the local population congregated to witness this new phenomenon. Aerophilatelic coverage of airport dedication ceremonies, however, did not take place in the greater Chicago area until 1928.

The first United States Post Office Department's sanctioned airmail flights in the Chicago area were staged at Cicero Field on Memorial Day week-end, 1912. Between May 30 and June 2, flights were made between Cicero, Elmhurst and Wheaton. Pioneer pilots Max Lillie and Paul Studensky made the runs, carrying a total of 485 pounds of mail over the four-day period.

On May 23, 1918, Katherine Stinson, the first woman airmail pilot, flew sixty pieces of mail on a special flight from Grant Park to New York City.

Covers were postmarked in Chicago and show a black cachet "Aerial Mail Service." During this flight, she broke two American records, one for non-stop distance, the other for endurance. Due to many complications, her flight took two days, but it did establish the feasibility of a regular airmail service.

The first Government Flights took place on May 15, 1918, between Washington, Philadelphia, and New York City. On September 5, 1918, Army pilots Max Miller and Ed W. Gardner left New York for Chicago in Army planes, carrying about 50 pounds of mail. After some mishaps along the route, Miller was forced down in Lock Haven while Gardner landed at Grant Park after 23 hours and 55 minutes flying time.

The first airport in the Chicago area to serve as a postal station on a regular basis was Grant Park. On May 15, 1919, the first leg of the trans-continental airmail route from New York to Chicago was inaugurated. To establish the second leg from Chicago to Omaha, Nebraska, an experimental flight left Grant Park on January 8, 1920, with a small amount of mail. The long-awaited trans-continental airmail route was inaugurated on September 8, 1920, with a flight from Mineola, Long Island, to San Francisco.

Grant Park is located in downtown Chicago, near the business district. Its main purpose was that of a park. Aviation facilities were never envisioned there. Therefore the Post Office Department shifted its Chicago airmail operations in 1920 to suburban Maywood, where two new airports had been built: Ashburn and Checkerboard Field. The United States Post Office Department's Airmail Service used Checkerboard Field until a fire in 1921 destroyed most of the buildings. They then moved across the street to some government owned land and constructed Maywood Airfield. Indeed this terminal was named the hub of airmail facilities for the whole country.

Chicago's political leaders had come to the conclusion that if the city was going to become a major aviation center, as it was a railroad center, and had been a shipping center, the city needed to build and operate a modern airport.

The Kelly Act of 1925 required the Post Office to turn over its mail service to private contractors, providing for Contract Air Mail (CAM).

On April 1, 1925, the Chicago City Council approved a 25-year lease for a new airport site. Chicago Municipal Airport, later named Midway Airport, opened on May 8, 1926. Within a few years, it become the world's busiest airport. All airmail handling was transferred in 1927 from Maywood Field.

**Table 1:
Chicago Area
Public Use
Airports – 1931**

4	Ashburn
5	Ashton (Aux)
6	Aurora
62	Aurora (Dept of Commerce)
	Chicago-Aero Club
	Chicago-Cook County
	Chicago-Lincoln
	Chicago-Morton Grove
	Chicago-Southtown
	Chicago-Checkerboard
9	Chicago-Westchester
10	Chicago-Elmhurst
11	Chicago-Lansing (Ford)
12	Chicago Municipal (Midway)
14	Gary
15	Glenview Curtiss-Reynolds
18	Chicago Harlem (Oaklawn)
	Hinckley-Eagle
22	Joliet Municipal
	Lombard
	Marengo-Kelley
27	McCool (Dep of Commerce)
29	Pal-Wauke, Des Plaines
32	Ravenswood, Des Plaines
35	St. Charles, DuPag)
37	Sky Harbor, Northbrook
41	Stinson La Grange (McCook)
45	Waukegan, Lake Co
46	Wheeling-Des Plaines(Aux)
	Wheaton-Cantigny
48	Will County
49	Chicago Wilson
52	Yorkville

Table 1 lists all public use airports in the greater Chicago area, as they were published in the *Pilots Handbook, 1931*. The numbers in front of some of these airports correspond to the numbers used in Figures 7 and 8, taken from *Metro-Chicago Airports*, a 1984 publication by the Illinois Department of Aeronautics.

In 1929, a 65-acre site northwest of Chicago, Orchard Park Airfield, was donated to Chicago City Council as the site of the "airport of the future." It was used for a while in the 1940s by the Douglas Aircraft Company, building transport planes for the war effort.

This "insignificant" airfield and the surrounding site was purchased from the Army and formally dedicated on June 22, 1949 (Figure 1). It was named for the first pilot to lose his life in World War II, Navy Lieutenant Comander Edward "Butch" O'Hare.

O'Hare International Airport grew to become reputedly the world's largest and busiest airport. The O'Hare Airport Mail Facilities were dedicated on July 4, 1955.

Up to the time of the inauguration of service at Midway Airport, there were no airport dedication ceremonies in the greater Chicago area. The first dedication ceremony with a souvenir cover was in 1928 in Belvidere, near Rockford. Since that time, there have been many official airport dedications.

On May 15, 1938, during the National Airmail Week celebration, Chicago was one of the first cities to embrace autogiro mail. The wing-less rotorcraft, painted with the colors of Trans World Airlines, TWA, departed from the roof of the downtown post office with 78 pounds of mail for the Chicago Municipal Airport (Midway). The return flight to the post office left about half an hour later.

Occasionally the site or the nature of a first flight is something more than a standard affair. Sometimes the flight does not even take place at an airfield. An ordinary cover can conceal the unexpected. Figure 2 shows such an example.

Figure 1: O'Hare Airport Dedication cover, 1949, prepared by the Jack Knight Air Mail Society (Nancy Blouin collection).

Figure 2: National Airmail Week celebration at Brookfield Zoo. Carried by Pony Express to the mail plane, then flown from the zoo grounds to Chicago Municipal Airport (Courtesy Brookfield Historical Society Archives).

On May 19, 1938, the town of Brookfield, a south-west suburb of Chicago, created a most unusual first flight as part of the National Air Mail Week celebration. On that date, 3,320 covers were collected at the nearby post offices of Brookfield, Riverside, Congress Park, and Hollywood. Taking part in this aviation ceremony was Mei-Mei, the giant panda residing at the zoo, and a pony express team which delivered the souvenir mail to the "flying field," the parking lot of the Brookfield Zoo. A Cessna airplane then flew the mail to Chicago's Municipal Airport from where it was forwarded to its destination.

In an effort to move the mails faster between points in Chicago and the surrounding suburbs, the use of helicopters was seen as a near perfect solution because they could land on building tops and in small fields. Added to this was the incentive of the new 5-cent airmail rate. The first experimental flights of this type took place in the Los Angeles, California, area in July 1946, but the first flight over Chicago took on a novel twist.

Figure 3: Experimental Helicopter flight from downtown Chicago to the suburbs (Evanston).

On October 1, 1946, a Sikorsky R-5-D type helicopter lifted off from the roof of the Merchandise Mart, the largest (at the time) office building in the world. All flights first went west to Berwyn and Oak Park, then north to Glenview, and then east to Evanston, to continue to Des Plaines. It was the stop in Evanston which proved to be the most interesting of the route. Originally, no landing was planned. The aircraft was to hover over the playing field of the Dyche Stadium at Northwestern University. Instead, to the delight of the small crowd which was there mainly for the sporting event, the football game came to a halt as fans and players watched the "aerial elevator" set down on a large "X" on the field (Figure 3).

Eventually, on September 19, 1949, a regular airmail service (AM96) using helicopters was instituted which basically followed the experimental flight route. This route never lived up to the original expectations, but a much reduced service continued until December 31, 1965.

Meigs Field, an airport in the middle of town, not too far away from Grant Park, is the third airport operated by the City of Chicago. It is situated on what used to be called Northerly Island, the only man made island off the Chicago Lakefront. This area was first used during the Century of Progress Exhibition in 1933-34.

The facility was opened on December 10, 1948, and within seven years, it became the busiest single runway airport in the world, serving the downtown Chicago business community.

On June 30, 1949, the name of this lakefront airport was changed to Merrill C. Meigs Field, in honor of the Chicago pioneer pilot and former chairman of the Chicago Aero Commission. It was dedicated a year later (Figure 4).

Figure 4: Dedication of Merrill C. Meigs Field, June 30, 1950.

Airport dedications and re-dedications remained a frequent affair well into the 1950s and 1960s. By this time however, urban sprawl made the building of new airports, even small ones, less and less of a possibility.

Now that Chicago's O'Hare and Midway Airports are proving to be inadequate for the future of air traffic, the city and state are looking for a third major airport. When and if this will come about, this new airport of the future will have the largest airport dedication ceremony since O'Hare in 1949.

From the beginning of airport dedications, the Chicago Metropolitan Region was represented aerophilatelically and this continues up to this day. Following is a listing of philatelically commemorated airport dedications in this greater Chicago Metropolitan Region which includes the City of Chicago and its suburbs, a six county area in Northeastern Illinois, and a two county area in the Northwestern Indiana Metropolitan Region.

Most of the data presented in the table was taken from the American Air Mail Catalogues, with additional information added from Jack Knight Air Mail Society archives.

Airport Dedications in the Chicago Metropolitan Region, commemorated with souvenir covers.

1928	Nov 10	Belvidere	Three-line cachet
1929	Jun 1	Cary	Cachet with or without inscription of Cary Aviation Co. (50)
	Jun 2	Cary	same (50), postmarked Jun 3
	Oct 20	Glenview	Curtiss-Reynolds (private) cachet (521) same cachet, but postmarked on Oct 21
	Oct 27	Arlington Heights	Postmaster inscription (39)
1930	Jun 8	Harlem	Cachet not recorded
	Jun 10	Elgin	Airplane cachet by Exchange Club and Chamber of Commerce Printed letter "E" design cachet by management
	Jun 18	Gary, Indiana	Indiana Air Tour cachet (171)
	Jul 4	Hinckley	Inscription by Eagle Airways Dedication ceremonies continued on Jul 5 and 6, but no covers are known
	Sep 6	Joliet Municipal	Chamber of Commerce cachet
	Sep 7	Joliet Municipal	same
1931	Sep 5	Lansing	Skeeter Airport Printed cachet by Legion (34) same, postmarked Hammond, IN (24) Printed cachet by Legion "Welcomes Capt. von Gronau"

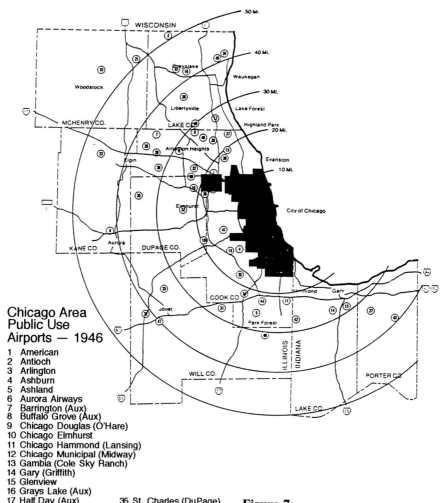

Chicago Area
Public Use
Airports — 1946

1 American
2 Antioch
3 Arlington
4 Ashburn
5 Ashland
6 Aurora Airways
7 Barrington (Aux)
8 Buffalo Grove (Aux)
9 Chicago Douglas (O'Hare)
10 Chicago Elmhurst
11 Chicago Hammond (Lansing)
12 Chicago Municipal (Midway)
13 Gambia (Cole Sky Ranch)
14 Gary (Griffith)
15 Glenview
16 Grays Lake (Aux)
17 Half Day (Aux)
18 Harlem
19 Hinsdale
20 Howell Blue Island
21 Johnsburg
22 Joliet Municipal
23 Kane County
24 Lake County
25 Lewis-Lockport
26 Libertyville
27 McCool Intermediate
28 Murphys Circus (Aux)
29 Pal-Waukee
30 Pralls Pits (Aux)
31 Prosperi
32 Ravenswood
33 Round Lake
34 Rubinkam

35 St. Charles (DuPage)
36 Schaumburg (Aux)
37 Sky Harbor
38 Sky Haven
39 Skyway
40 Spoerlein (Aux)
41 Stinson
42 Triangle
43 Urschel
44 Washington Park
45 Waukegan (Lake Co)
46 Wheeling (Aux)
47 Wilhelmi-Joliet
48 Will County
49 Wilson
50 Woodale
51 Woodstock
52 York Township

Figure 7:
Chicago Airports — 1946

In 1946 there were 47 airports in the Illinois six county area and five airports in Indiana to serve the needs of both commercial and general aviation. The average distance between airports and the Chicago central business district was 26 miles in Illinois, 34 miles in Indiana.

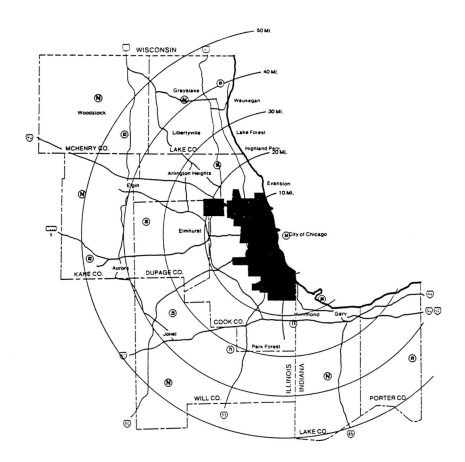

Chicago Area Public Use Airports of the Future — 2000

 9 Chicago Douglas (O'Hare)
11 Chicago Hammond (Lansing)
12 Chicago Municipal (Midway)
25 Lewis-Lockport
35 St. Charles (DuPage)
54 Chicago-Meigs
58 Pal-Waukee (Priester)
61 Waukegan Memorial
62 Aurora Municipal
63 Crystal Lake
71 Frankfort
62 Aurora Municipal
80 Gary Municipal
81 Porter County

Figure 8:
Chicago Area Airports —
Recommendations for the future

Studies made by the Illinois Division of Aeronautics and the Federal Aviation Administration predict that only 12 of today's 26 airports will be in operation by the year 2000. These 12 airports will have a capacity shortfall of 1.7 million operations per year. To handle air traffic in the year 2000, it will be necessary to construct five additional general aviation airports in the region, and expand many of those already in existence.

Chicago Metropolitan Region Airport Dedications (cont'd)

1931	Sep 6	Lansing	same (32)
	Sep 7	Lansing	same (32)
	Nov 15	Chicago Municipal	Chicago Airmail Society cachet, postmarked Air Mail Field (57)
1933	Sep 5	South Bend	Bendix Municipal Airport, Chamber of Commerce cachet (125)
1934	Oct 28	Joliet	Re-Dedication of Municipal Airport Chamber of Commerce sticker cachet (about 200)
			same, but postmarked Oct 29
1937	Aug 28	Glenview	Dedication of Curtiss-Reynolds Airport, Naval Reserve Aviation Base Circular cachet by Navy and Chamber of Commerce (243)
	Aug 28	Glenview	a) same plus four-line printed (60) or typed (9) over stamped plane or airship by Evanston Philatelic Society
1937	Aug 28	Glenview	b) without Chamber of Commerce cachet, with 4- line printed (460) or typed (12) over rubber stamped plane or dirigible by Evanston Philatelic Society, postmarked Evanston
			c) without Chamber of Commerce cachet, but with inscription signed by Cmdr. RalphWoods, postmarked Hawthorne Sta. Chicago (3)
			d) Chamber of Commerce cachet, plus 4-line black printed "Official opening, 28 August 1937 - etc" over larger stamped air plane, postmarked Glenview
1940	Sep 2	Lockport	Airport of Lewis School of Aeronautics, cachet by management, with or without "Carried by a glider." Flown to and post-marked at Chicago Air Mail Field (580)
			same, postmarked Lockport, IL (280)
			Some covers were postmarked Sep 3, due to Post Office error
1941	Jun 29	Chicago	Re-Dedication of Municipal Airport, with (280) or without (10) cachet by local Air-port Historical Society, AHS, member, postmarked Chicago Air Mail Field
1941	Aug 30	Elmhurst	Cachet by AOPA (Aircraft Owners and Pilots Association) and others; postmarked Chicago (235)
			same, postmarked Elmhurst (105)
	Aug 31	Elmhurst	same, postmarked Chicago Air Mail Field (423)
	Sep 1	Elmhurst	same, postmarked Chicago Air Mail Field (490)

Chicago Metropolitan Region Airport Dedications (cont'd)

1941	Sep 1	Elmhurst	a) without cachet, but postmarked in Elmhurst (5) b) without cachet, but postmarked in Elmhurst on Sep 2
	Sep 21	Elgin	Kane County Airport, with Postmaster inscription (115)
1943	Jul 30	Park Ridge	Airport and Plant of Douglas Aircraft Company, with (154) or without (5) private cachet
1948	Dec 10	Chicago	Northerly Air Strip (now Meigs Field); Jack Knight Air Mail Society cachet, Air Mail Field postmark (329) with city postmark (252)
1949	Sep 18	Park Ridge	O'Hare Field; sticker cachet by Jack Knight Air Mail Society (65) same, flown to Chicago Air Mail Field (130)
1950	Jun 30	Chicago	Merrill C. Meigs Field; sticker cachet by Jack Knight Air Mail Society (277)
1958	Sep 13	Crystal Lake	Municipal Airport, Postmaster inscription (50)
	Oct 19	Gary, Indiana	Municipal Airport
1963	Mar 23	Chicago	O'Hare International, Re-Dedication (100)
1964	Jul 2	Chicago	Heliport (radio station WGM), covers flown to and postmarked at Airport Mail Facility O'Hare (15)
1964	Sep 5	Park Forest	Municipal Heliport (53)
1965	Jun 20	Kenosha	Municipal Airport
1967	May 31	Joliet	Silvercross Hospital Heliport (few)
	Oct 4	Chicago	Robin Dean Heliport, Cook County Hospital (100)
1968	Aug 23	Chicago	Martha Washington Hospital Heliport (77)
1969	Mar 15	Glenview	Naval Air Station, United States Coast Guard Glenview Air Station (10)
1974	May 25	Fox River Grove	Eagle's Nest Balloon Port (1,035)

Bibliography:

Archives of the Evanston and Brookfield Historical Societies.

Pilots Handbook 1931. Written, compiled, edited, and published by Pilots Handbook Publishing Co:.Los Angeles, California

CAMS Chicago Air Mail Society Bulletin, Miscellaneous issues, 1982 through today.

Haring, Robert E. and Dr. Perham C. Nahl et al. 1978. "U.S. Contract Air Mail Covers, Routes 73—299." Vol 3 ed 5: 1181-1184. *American Air Mail Catalogue.* Cinnaminson, New Jersey: American Air Mail Society.

Nahl, Dr. Perham C. et al. 1974. "U.S. Governmental Flights." Vol 1 ed 5: 53-96. *American Air Mail Catalogue.* Washington, DC: American Air Mail Society:

Scamehorn, Howard L. 1957. *Balloons to Jets, 1855-1955, A Century of Aeronautics in Illinois.* Illinois State Historical Society Occasional Publications No.52. Chicago, Illinois: Henry Regnery Comp.

Ware, Dick. 1984. *Metro Chicago Airports 2000.* Illinois Department of Transportation, Division of Aeronautics: Springfield, Illinois.

Wynn, William T. et al. 1978. "Airport Dedication Covers." Vol 3 ed 5: 1299-1408. *American Air Mail Catalogue.* Cinnaminson, New Jersey: American Air Mail Society:

Young, David and Neal Callahan. 1981. *Fill the Heavens with Commerce, Chicago Aviation, 1855-1926.* Chicago, Illinois: Chicago Review Press.

Raymond A. Broms is President of the Chicago Air Mail Society and editor of *Space Shuttle Era* in the *Jack Knight Air Log* and *AFA News.* He is a member of the Chicago Philatelic Society and promotes actively aero- and astrophilately with children in Chicagoland. His own collecting interests include space and rockets, Zeppelins, Sweden, and Pitcairn Island.

7

Canadian Airmails,

1918-1934

by Richard K. Malott

The development of Canada, particularly the vast expanses of land in northern areas, depended greatly upon aircraft. Communications among Canada's various regions were enhanced by the transfer of correspondence by air. The first recorded instances of airmail were ". . carried by a paper kyte" on March 18, 1848, and "Despatched by a Balloon, from *H.M.S. Assistance*" on June 10, 1853, as attempts were made to contact Sir John Franklin, lost in the Canadian Arctic.

Aircraft capabilities were enhanced by research and development during the First World War. The potential of the aircraft in breaching the vast distances of Canada and in delivering the mail improved in most areas of Canada. This article highlights many of the more significant flights in the develop-ment of airmail services in Canada up to 1934, as well as basic Canadian airmail rates.

Pioneer Airmail Flights of Canada

Canada's first official airmail flight was flown in a Curtiss JN-4 Can (Canuck) aircraft by Captain Brian A. Peck, a pilot of the Royal Flying Corps stationed at Leaside Camp, Ontario. It went from Montreal to Toronto on June 24, 1918. Along with the 124 specially cacheted envelopes (Figure 1) was a case of whisky for a wedding party at Leaside Camp, the original reason for the flight. The first class postage rate of 3 cents paid for the air service as there was no official Canadian airmail rate.

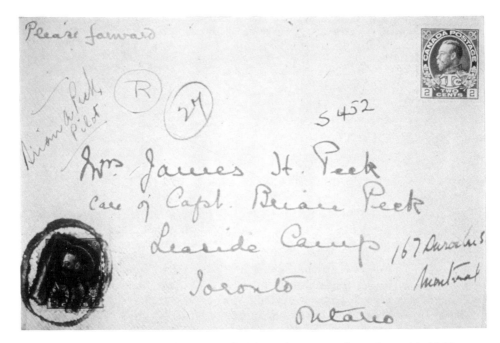

Figure 1: One of 124 letters carried by Brian A. Peck on June 24, 1918, from Montreal to Toronto, signed by Captain Peck. This cover is now part of the archives of the Canadian War Museum.

On July 9, 1918, the second official airmail flight was flown from the Exhibition Grounds near Calgary, Alberta, to Edmonton, Alberta. The famous American aviatrix, Katherine Stinson, flew 250 envelopes at the 3 cents rate in her Curtiss Stinson Special. Miss Stinson was the only woman to officially fly mail in Canada; she did so just 15 days after the first official mail was flown by Capt. Peck. The trip took her 2 hours and 5 minutes to fly the 175 miles, not counting an emergency landing.

From August 15 to September 4, 1918, three experimental flights were flown by RAF personnel from Toronto to Ottawa, and return. Most mail carried on the first flight was "official mail," mail flown on the other two flights required a special 25-cent vignette of the Aero Club of Canada affixed in addition to the 3 cents Canadian postage for first class mail. There was no official Canadian airmail rate, the first class postage rate of

3 cents paid for the transportation by air. One of the pilots was Lieutenant Arthur M. Dunstan, RAF, famous as the first airmail pilot in Canada to use a parachute to save his life after his aircraft ran out of gas in fog over Dunville, Ontario, in 1931.

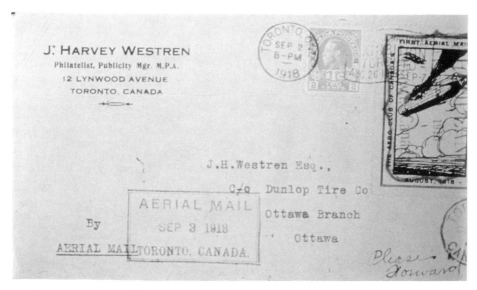

Figure 2: One of 43 letters flown on September 4, 1918 from Toronto to Ottawa by Lt. E. C. Burton. Letters carry the Aero Club of Canada vignette, without value imprinted, costing 25 cents.

Although the 1918 trial airmail flights proved successful, scheduled routes were not implemented in Canada until 1927. Between 1918 and 1927, there were many experimental and historic airmail flights in Canada, some requiring more special vignettes (Figure 2).

There were first flights in early 1919 by Eddie Hubbard (and William E. Boeing as passenger) between Vancouver and Seattle, as well as between Victoria, British Columbia, and Seattle, Washington. The Canadian Rockies were conquered by air by Captain Ernest C. Hoy flying a Curtiss JN-4 (Canuck) aircraft when he carried mail between Vancouver and Calgary and points in between on August 7, 1919. The return trip ended in a crash at Golden, British Columbia, on August 11. The Aero Club of Canada had special envelopes prepared and flown from Toronto to New York, and return on August 25, 1919, by Colonel W. Barker, V.C., the famous Canadian First World War fighter pilot ace (see Figure 3).

Figure 3: Two covers flown by Colonel W. Barker from Toronto to New York, August 25, 1919. It is not known how many pieces were carried, but the $1 charge for the vignette was to cover trip expenses.

The famous series of attempted flights from Newfoundland to England culminated in Captain John Alcock's and Lieutenant Arthur Whitten Brown's successful non-stop flight across the Atlantic on June 14, 1919. That Atlantic crossing prompted an attempted flight by Admiral Sir Mark Kerr on July 4, 1919, in the Handley Page four-engine bomber *The Atlantic* from St. John's, Newfoundland, to Mineola, New York. This new route, in lieu of flying over the Atlantic Ocean, was fortuitous for Admiral Kerr since an oil line broke and forced the large bomber, carrying a small amount of mail, down on a race track at Parrsboro, Nova Scotia. The resultant rough landing so damaged *The Atlantic* that it required three months to repair. On October 9, 1919, with more mail, *The Atlantic* took off for Mineola, New York. Again the aircraft was forced down, this time at Greenport, New York. The plane finally reached Mineola with a crew of eight and four newsmen, plus a few letters. The external postage rate was still 3 cents as an airmail rate had not yet been considered.

Additional flights were from New Brunswick to Prince Edward Island in September 1919; Dawson, Yukon Territory, to Fairbanks, Alaska, on August 18, 1920; a trans-Canada flight from October 7 through 27, 1920 by several pilots and different aircraft from Halifax, Nova Scotia, to Vancouver, British Columbia; Toronto to Hamilton and return for the

Grand Army of Canada Carnival flights by pilot Arthur K. Colley and mechanic Landigan on May 28, 1920. Upon Landigan's death, his brother destroyed several flown envelopes from this flight, making the remaining few covers some of Canada's scarcest flown airmail envelopes.

Experimental winter airmail flights between Toronto, Ontario, and the aviation field at Camp Borden, Ontario, were flown by Lieutenant A.C. McLerie from January to April 1921.

Other flights carrying mail were attempted from Lethbridge, Alberta, to Ottawa, Ontario, on June 22, 1922, and from Estevan, Saskatchewan, to Winnipeg, Manitoba, on October 1, 1924.

The trip from London, Ontario, to London, England, was unsuccessfully attempted by the undaunted ex-RAF pilots, Captain Terrance B. Tully and Lieutenant James V. Medcalf, in a Stinson SM-1 aircraft, during the period from August 29 through September 7, 1927.

Before leaving London, Ontario, for the second attempt on September 1, 1927, Dr. L. Seale Holmes, a prominent Canadian airmail collector with the assistance of the London Postmaster, removed one stamped, addressed and postmarked envelope as an example of the mail being carried, just in case the flight was not successful.

On the morning of September 7, 1927, the aircraft took off from Harbour Grace, Newfoundland, with the two pilots and a bag of mail. The aircraft flew into eternity with no trace ever being found of the pilots, aircraft, or its contents.

CANADIAN PACIFIC RAILWAY COMPANY'S TELEGRAPH

TELEGRAM

27RNXA 23   HARBORGRACE NFLD SEPT 7-27

ANNE L TULLY
          CARE ARTHUR LONDON
WE ARE JUST OFF ON A LONG PATROL TODAY YOU SHOULD
HEAR FROM US THIS TIME TOMORROW LOVE TO YOU
TERRY AND PAT.
          TERANCE.   905A

Figure 4: This historic telegram sent from Harbour Grace, Newfoundland, on September 7, 1927, is a significant historical document in Canada's airmail history.

Tully and Medcalf announced their departure on September 7 with a telegram (Figure 4), promising to telegraph upon arrival in England. There was no second telegram and thus the envelope removed from the mailbag in London, Ontario became Canada's rarest flown airmail envelope.

These and other early flown envelopes constitute the pioneer airmails of Canada.

Semi-Official Airmail Flights of Canada

The era of the bush pilots in Canada began in late 1924 and early 1925, when the demand for fast, reasonably safe, and not too expensive flights into isolated areas of Canada's northlands, hinterlands and mountainous areas arose as a result of geology research and the discovery of gold in Northern Ontario and Northern Quebec.

Pilots flew all types of cargo into these areas: prospectors, dogs, supplies of all kinds, canoes, and — as a courtesy — private mail. Pilots who put all their life savings into these aviation companies needed revenue from any and all sources.

The desire for speedy correspondence was identified as a sure source of income, and thus the semi-official airmail stamps came into being.

Anyone wishing to use the airline's airmail service purchased a semi-official airmail vignette from the airline, costing from 5 cents to $1.00, in addition to the normal postage stamp for the Canadian Government Post Office's first class mail rate. There was no airmail rate until August 24, 1928, and no official airmail stamp until September 21, 1928, when a 5-cent airmail stamp was issued.

There were at least sixteen aviation companies known to have printed their own semi-official airmail stamps. Some companies printed only one stamp, while others printed at least sixteen varieties.

These companies served almost all the different regions of Canada until they were amalgamated into two large companies in the late 1930s — Trans Canada Air Lines (now Air Canada) and Canadian Pacific Airlines (now Canadian Airlines International).

It should be noted that the 5-cent airmail rate was not charged for letters carried by the companies authorized to issue semi-official airmail stamps. Those letters needed only the payment of first class postage in effect at date of mailing.

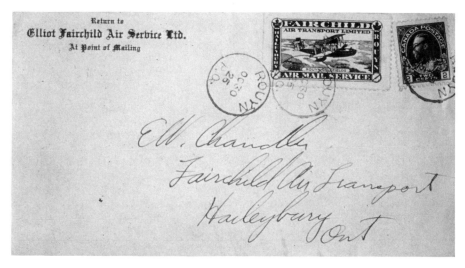

Figure 5: A Fairchild Air Transport Ltd. flown cover with the blue vignette and the 2 cents Canadian Post Office rate, postmarked October, 1925.

The first daring airline to commence airmail business was Laurentide Air Services, Ltd., on September 21, 1924, between Haileybury, Ontario, and Rouyn, Quebec. This company carried out forestry fire patrols, flew prospectors into the northern gold fields, and carried a considerable amount of mail and parcels. They issued two green and two red semi-official stamps under Canada's Post Office authorization.

The navigation and radio aids were almost non-existent, the weather was bad, and aircraft maintenance quite difficult to perform. Despite these serious problems determined bush pilots, such as C.H. "Punch" Dickens and A.H. Farrington, got the mail through.

In order to give as complete a picture as possible, the semi-official airmail companies that operated in the years between 1924 through 1934, are presented in the following table, showing some of the basic information on each company, with routes and areas served.

Canadian Semi-Official Airmail Companies

Company Name	Stamps issued	First Flight (date)	First Flights and area served
Laurentide Air Service, Ltd	4	Sep 21, 1924	Haileybury, Ontario to Rouyn, Quebec
Northern Air Service, Ltd	1	May 18, 1925	Haileybury to Rouyn
Jack V. Elliot Air Service	2	Mar 6, 1926	Rolling Portage to Red Lake, Ontario Sioux Lookout, Ontario
Elliot-Fairchild Air Service	2	Apr 15, 1926	Rolling Portage to Red Lake Red Lake District of Ontario
Elliot-Fairchild Air Transport, Ltd	1	Aug 13, 1926	Haileybury, Ontario to Rouyn, Quebec Quebec goldfields
Fairchild Air Transport, Ltd	1	Oct 20, 1926	Haileybury, Ontario, to Rouyn, Quebec Northern Ontario goldfields
Patricia Airways & Exploration, Ltd	16 [*1]	Jun 27, 1926	Sioux Lookout to Red Lake District includes Pine Ridge, Birch Lake, Woman Lake, Hailey bury and Rouyn West Ontario goldfields
Western Canada Airways, Ltd	2	May 10, 1927	Rolling Portage to Gold Pines, Ontario. Red Lake District, Ontario North West Territories and Winnipeg area, 1,500 miles up Mackenzie River to Arctic, West Ontario goldfields
Yukon Airways & Exploration, Ltd	1	Oct 24 - Nov 24, 1927	Whitehorse to Mayo Landing Dawson, Wernecke, Keno Hill, and Aklavik, all in the Yukon Yukon Territory, but also south to British Columbia

*1] There are many varieties of these issues due to various overprints being made in various color of ink, by inverting and by doubling the overprints. Most of these were done deliberately.

Figure 6: A flown cover with Western Canada Airways semi-official stamp issued to commemorate the 60th anniversary of the Confederation, July 1, 1927, and that stamp could be used only on that one day.

Figure 7: A Patricia Airways and Exploration Company, Ltd. flown cover with the 50 cents blue vignette and the 2 cents Canadian Post Office rate.

Canadian Semi-Official Airmail Companies (cont'd)

Company Name	Stamps issued	First Flight (date)	First Flights and area served
Patricia Airways, Ltd	1	Feb 4, 1928	Sioux Lookout to Gold Pines, Red Lake, Clearwater, Jackson Manion and Narrow Lake, Ontario Western Ontario areas, in general, same as P.A.&E.
British Columbia Airways, Ltd (started as a flying school in 1927)	1	Jul 23, 1928	Victoria to Vancouver, British Columbia Victoria and Vancouver area
Klondike Airways, Ltd	1	Oct 13, 1928	Whitehorse to Wernecke, Keno Hill and Mayo Landing Yukon Territory
Commercial Airways, Ltd	4 [*2]	May 21, 1929	Edmonton, Alberta to Grand Prairie and return. Northern Alberta and North West Territory
Cherry Red Airlines, Ltd	1 [*3]	Jul 3, 1929	Prince Albert to Rottenstone Lake, Lac La Ronge and return Northern Saskatchewan area
Canadian Airways, Ltd	2 [*3]	Dec 30, 1932	Edmonton, Alberta to Fort McMurray, North West Territories Northern Alberta, North West Territories,Red Lake goldfields in Ontario, Winnipeg area

*2] Many varieties of printing and overprinting, paper and perforation, exist from this,as well as from other airlines.

*3] Cherry Red Airlines issued two stamps, one regular and one as an overprint variety.

For the record only: Maritime and Newfoundland Airways operated in 1930 on the island of Cape Breton, in Nova Scotia, St. Pierre et Miquelon (French possession), and Newfoundland. At least six stamp issues were printed, but the mail was not authorized to be flown.

Other Special Event Flights

During the overlapping period of the pioneer and semi-official airmail flights, various special events flights took place into or from Canada for which souvenir mail was prepared and flown. Some of these events are listed below.

- New York, Toronto and Red Lake from March 27 to April 12, 1926,by Patricia Airways and Exploration Company, Ltd. in a Curtiss Lark and piloted by Captain Roy Maxwell.

- Ottawa to Vancouver transcontinental flight by Squadron Leader A.E. Godfrey, RCAF, to prove the feasibility of regular aircraft routes across Canada. There were 300 cacheted envelopes flown on this flight stopping at various locations en route to Vancouver, British Columbia, from September 5 to 8, 1928.

- The MacAlpine Rescue Search, Fort Resolution, Bathurst Inlet and The Pas, November 2 through December 4, 1929. During the search over the Arctic for the lost MacAlpine Party, the lead search pilot, Andrew Cruickshank, carried with him seventeen envelopes postmarked at Fort Resolution on November 2, 1929. The search was successful.

- The visit of the airship *R 100* from Cardington, England, to Montreal, Quebec, July 29 through August 13, 1930. Souvenir mail was postmarked in Montreal between August 1 and 13, but only three courtesy flown covers for the return flight, August 13 to 16, 1930, are known and verified.

- The flight of General Italo Balbo from Rome to Chicago and return via Shediac, New Brunswick, and Montreal, Quebec, July 14 through 25, 1933. The Italian aircraft armada was attending the Century of Progress Exposition at Chicago and carried specially prepared Canadian envelopes, flown from Shediac and Montreal to Chicago and then back to Rome, Italy. The special rate charged by General Balbo was $4.50 from Newfoundland and $1.45 from Canada.

The development of Canadian airmail services did not stop in 1934. The Canadian Post Office promoted airmail services by issuing special announcements for the new airmail routes and by providing special cachets. Hundreds of different types of cacheted first flight covers were prepared in quantities of several thousands each from 1925 to 1948. But that is another story.

Bibliography

Smith, O. W. R.. 1929. *Air Mail Catalogue Canada and Newfoundland.* Gordon Crouch and Fred Jarrett. Toronto: Marks Stamp Company.

Morgan, Ian C. 1931. *The Specialized Catalogue of Canadian Air Mails.* Montreal: Century Stamp Co.

Harmer, Cyril H. C. et al. 1981. "Newfoundland and the Labrador, First and Special Flights." *The American Air Mail Catalogue* Vol 4 ed 5: 1635-1648. Cinnaminson, New Jersey: The American Air Mail Society.

Malott, Major Richard K. (Ret'd) et al. 1981. "Canada. Pioneer Flights, Semi-official first and special flights, Official Governmental Flights, Airmail services, Air stage services." *The American Air Mail Catalogue* Vol 4 ed 5: 1651-1741. Cinnaminson, New Jersey: The American Air Mail Society.

Holmes, Dr. L. Seale Associates. 1968. *Specialized Philatelic Catalogue of Canada and British North America* ed 10. Toronto: Ryerson Press.

Dalwick, R. E. R. and Cyril H. C. Harmer. 1984 *Newfoundland Air Mails, 1919-1939. (An Update of 1953 Edition).* Cinnaminson, New Jersey: The American Air Mail Society.

Editorial help for this article was given by Basil Burrell.

Major Richard K. Malott (Ret'd) is Vice-President and editor of the Canadian Aerophilatelic Society and a director of the Royal Philatelic Society of Canada. In 1974, he retired from the Canadian Armed Forces to assume the position of the Chief Curator of Collections at the Canadian War Museum in Ottawa, Canada. He plans to retire at the end 1992 after 42 years of government service. He collects, researches, exhibits and writes about Canadian airmails, crash covers, and aerogrammes.

8

Origins and Rates of the North Atlantic German Catapult Airmail

by **James W. Graue**

In the development of trans-oceanic airmail service, one of the most interesting approaches was the catapult airmail.

On July 22, 1929, the Deutsche Lufthansa inaugurated catapult airmail service from the passenger liner *D. Bremen* of the North German Lloyd line. A floatplane was catapulted from the ship when it was some distance out from New York (westbound) or Southampton (eastbound) to fly the mail ahead and thereby advance its delivery. The catapult flights from the German liners (service from the *D. Europa* was added in 1930) were made during the May to October season through 1935.

Supplementary mail flights from Köln, Germany, and Basel, Switzerland, to the ship at Cherbourg, France, provided further acceleration to the airmail. With the introduction of scheduled commercial Zeppelin airship service to North America in 1936, the catapult airmail service was discontinued.

The catapult airmails were and are highly collectible. The mail was marked with distinctive flight cachets which varied widely in design over the years and made it attractive.

More importantly, the catapult flights represented the first consistent means of advancing trans-North Atlantic mail delivery by the use of airplanes.

This article is limited to a discussion of the origins of German North Atlantic catapult airmail, as usually recognized by aerophilatelists, and their applicable postal rates.

I — Origins

The origins of the catapult airmails include . . .

I — 1. Inland Mail

Mail posted at or through inland offices in Germany or the United States. This is a broad classification which includes all origins other than seapost from the catapult flight ship.

Special recognition is given to certain unusual "inland" origins, for instance, the LZ127 *Graf Zeppelin* airship or seapost from other ships.

Purely commercial origins (from banks, commercial firms or other business operations) bear special mention. These are very few in number (in spite of the proven record of advanced delivery utilizing the catapult airmail service), attributed to the irregular schedule and seasonal availability. The common practice of discarding commercial covers contributed to its attrition.

Commercial catapult airmail is to be highly prized (Figure 1).

I — 2. Inland Plus Supplementary Flight Mail

Although this is an inland origin, the importance of the supplementary flights has prompted special recognition of the mails thus flown.

Figure 1: German commercial (inland origin) catapult cover.

Figure 2: German seapost catapult cover from a passenger on the steamer *D. Bremen* to Switzerland.

Special red cachets were applied to mails flown on the supplementary flights from Köln, but no markings were used on mail flown from Basel.

I — 3. Seapost

Mail posted on board the ship from which the catapult flight was made. Seapost from other ships passed through an inland office and is thus considered a special type of inland origin.

There are two types to be noted:

I — 3A. Deutsch — Amerikanische Seepost

German—American Seapost originating on board the catapult ships at sea or in their German port, Bremerhaven (Figure 2).

It was not unusual for collectors to send covers to the ship to be canceled with the seapost cancelers during the trip. For a period during 1933, German covers thus received a marking *Aufgabeort*, giving the city of origin, a practice which sharply separated the seapost mail posted by the passengers or crew from that sent in by collectors (Figure 3).

I — 3B. United States — German Seapost

Seapost originating on board the ships while in their American port (New York) or in American waters. The post office on these ships carried United States stamps to be used for this (Figure 4).

There were instances when mail bearing United States stamps was postmarked with the German "Deutsch-Amerikanische Seepost" canceler, but they are few in number.

Figure 3: Catapult flight cover with German seapost cancellations and *Aufgabeort* marking showing actual origin as Assel near Stade.

Figure 4: United States — German Seapost cover from the *D. Europa*.

II — Foreign Acceptances

Foreign acceptances are inland mails, but they command special interest because of their foreign origin and the fact that many of them were few in number.

Foreign acceptances include . . .

II — 1. Treaty States Mail (*Vertragsstaaten*)

Mail from nations that had formal agreements with Germany for the acceptance of their mail for catapult flight service (Figure 5).

Treaty State	Year	Treaty State	Year
Austria	1930-1931,	Liechtenstein	1930-1935
Austria	1934-1935	Luxembourg	1930-1935
Danzig	1929-1935	Netherlands	1931-1935
Denmark	1931-1935	Saar	1930-1935
Estonia	1934-1935	Switzerland	1929-1935
Hungary	1931-1935		

Luxembourg is unusual because its mixed franking are official. Luxembourg had special arrangements with the neighboring nations for the acceptance of its airmail if the airmail surcharges were paid in the stamps of the nation providing the airmail service. The first catapult airmail from Luxembourg was in 1930.

II — 2. Courtesy Acceptances Mail (*Mitläufer*)

Catapult airmail of non-participating countries, or non-treaty nations, was accepted in small numbers as a courtesy. The courtesy acceptances can be further divided into . .

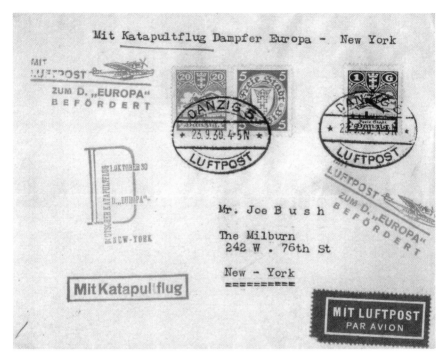

Figure 5. Danzig (treaty state) supplementary flight and catapult flight cover.

- Courtesy Acceptances — Pure: Those which bore only the stamps of the nation of origin, and
- Courtesy Acceptances — Mixed: Those which bore postage from the country of origin, in conjunction with (=mixed) the catapult airmail surcharges in German stamps or in United States stamps (Figure 6).

The covers of some nations can be found in both forms (e.g., Russia, Czechoslovakia, Canada, and Spain), while others will always be either pure or mixed.

Figure 6: Courtesy acceptance of mixed franking from Sweden.

The actual status of the catapult airmails of a few nations is uncertain, with the references in conflict. The Baltic nations are a case in point.

- Estonia has pure acceptances prior to 1934, its status as a treaty state begins in 1934.

- Latvia has pure acceptances from 1933 to 1935, but they are all courtesy acceptances.

- Lithuania is extremely scarce, and although referred to as a treaty state in the contemporary Kayssner catalog, it is referenced as a courtesy acceptance in later editions and modern references.

III — Rates

The rates for catapult airmail are generally the sum of the rates for international surface mail, special services (if any) and the surcharge rates for airmail services (supplementary flight from the continent to the steamer or catapult flight from the steamer to the continent).

III — 1. Germany

Airmail rates from Germany to other nations, via the United States, varied.

Registered mail was first accepted in 1931.

The special delivery rate is the international rate, which applied to all German seapost mail, posted on board the ship, directed to destinations in Germany.

Note that the airmail service in and beyond the United States required additional postage. This was true for both incoming and outgoing (see next page) catapult airmail. In Europe, however, airmail service was included in the catapult airmail rate, again for both incoming and outgoing mail.

Rates from Germany

BASIC INTERNATIONAL RATES May 1, 1929 — 1935	Printed Matter, per 50 g	5 Pfg
	up to 2 kg	5 Pfg
	Post card	15 Pfg
	Letter, first 20 g	25 Pfg
	each additional 20 g	
	or fraction thereof	15 Pfg
	Registration	30 Pfg
	Special Delivery	50 Pfg
SURCHARGE RATES for Airmail Service 1929 — 1934	Catapult flight, per 20 g	50 Pfg
	Supplementary flight,	
	per 20 g	30 Pfg
1935	Catapult flight, per 20 g	25 Pfg
	Supplementary flight,	
	per 20 g	15 Pfg
AIRMAIL in the United States (minimum rate) [*] May, 1929 — Feb 1931	Postcard	50 Pfg
	Letter, up to 20 g	50 Pfg
Mar 1931 — Apr 1933	Postcard	25 Pfg
	Letter, up to 20 g	25 Pfg
May 1933 — Apr 1934	Postcard	20 Pfg
	Letter, up to 20 g	20 Pfg
May 1934 — 1935	Postcard	15 Pfg
	Letter, up to 20 g	15 Pfg

* Note: Additional postage was required for letters weighing more than five grams.

III — 2. United States

The United States airmail rates for foreign destinations were apparently not well known, and much—if not most—of the United States inland airmail service catapult mail is overpaid. Domestic airmail surcharge rates were paid rather than the lesser surcharge for an international letter or the lesser combined rate initiated in 1932.

Rates from the United States

BASIC INTERNATIONAL RATES
 	
May 1, 1929 — 1934
	Printed Matter
	Post card
	Letter, first ounce
	  each additional ounce or
	  fraction thereof
	Registration
		1.5¢
		3¢
		5¢
		
		3¢
		15¢

SURCHARGE RATES for
  Airmail Service
  1929—1933
1934
1935
	Catapult flight, per half ounce
	
	Catapult flight, per half ounce
	Catapult flight, per half ounce
		15¢
		
		25¢
		20¢

AIRMAIL in the United States
  (minimum rate)
  Aug 1, 1928 — Jul 5, 1932
 	
Jul 6, 1932 — Nov 22, 1934
 	
Nov 23, 1934 —
  Jun 20, 1938
	Post card and
	  letter up to one ounce
	
	Combined rate * per first
	  ounce,
	  each additional ounce,
	  or fraction thereof
	Combined rate * per one
	  ounce or fraction
		4¢
		
		10¢
		
		15¢
		
		8¢

*Note: Combined rates include the basic international rate plus airmail within the United States.

Registered United States catapult airmail is relatively scarce.

III — 3. Foreign Acceptances

The catapult airmail rates for the various foreign nations which used the catapult airmail service, either by treaty or as a courtesy, are not well documented. Studies and surveys of these mails have been made but they are not always conclusive for a number of reasons.

The majority of catapult airmail, particularly the foreign origins, was philatelic, not commercial, and the preparers of the philatelic mails did not always feel constrained to adhere strictly to the required rates.

The number of rate variables make it difficult to secure the numbers of any one necessary to pin down the rate conclusively. Rates could change from year to year, or even in midyear.

In many instances, the stamps being used were a primary consideration, and the total bears no relationship to the required rate.

In spite of the problems, however, some of the rates of the treaty nations have been determined, either from documentation or by survey.

These rates and those of the nations which had courtesy acceptances are the subject of ongoing study by specialists. The rates of the courtesy acceptance nations are quite difficult to establish in the absence of official documentation because there are not many examples to draw on, especially for specific types and times.

The Kayssner *Catalogue of German Catapult Flights* of 1933 makes specific reference to the rates of Lithuania in noting its first acceptance in September, 1932:

> "The very high surcharge fees charged for catapult and supple-
> mentary airmail services from the treaty state Lithuania amounted
> to 7.90 Litas. This was in addition to the standard postal rates of
> 36 Ct for postal cards, 60 Ct for letters, 12 Ct for printed matter,
> and 60 Ct for registration."

Lithuania is one of the scarcest catapult flight origins, undoubtedly due in no small part to the high postage rate (Figure 8).

Foreign Acceptances: Rates

Country	Year	Post Card	Letter
Austria	1930	94 Gr	1.90 Sch
	1935	1.15 Sch *	
Danzig	1929	1.50 Gr	
	1930-1935	1.10 Gr	1.25 Gr
Denmark	1931		1.50 Kr *
	1933	1.00 Kr	
	1934	1.10 Kr	
Liechtenstein	1932-1933	70 Rp	80 Rp
Netherlands	1931-1934	57.5 Ct	62.5 Ct
	1935	47.5 Ct	52.5 Ct
Saar	1930-1933	2.90 Fr	4.50 Fr
Switzerland	1929	2.00 SFr	2.05 SFr
	1930-1931	1.25 SFr	1.30 SFr
	1932-1933	0.75 SFr	0.80 SFr
	1934	0.85 SFr	0.90 SFr
	1935	0.50 SFr	0.55 SFr

* Note: Supplementary flight was included

Figure 7: United States registered inland cover from St. Louis with correct 39 cents rate: international surface rate, 5 cents; surcharge for airmail in the United States, 4 cents; catapult flight, 15 cents; registration 15 cents

Conclusion

It is the 1936 edition of the *Kayssner* catalog which tells the ending of the catapult flight era best. The following passage from the introduction expresses apprehension and hope:

" . . . the new airship LZ129 will carry trans-Atlantic mail at regular intervals. Time alone will tell to what extent the catapult airmails will be used in the future. A drop is hardly expected, as the postage is sure to be cheaper than that of the airship."

But the final page, entered as the catalog went to press, spelled the end:

". . . we are informed that in optima forma the catapult flights have come to an end. The public notice sounds:

"Flights in advance from the steamers *Bremen* and *Europa* on their voyages to America will not take place any longer, as the airship *Hindenburg* will undertake a number of passages to the United States of America during the months of May to October, and therefore will be used as means for the conveyance of mail."

Figure 8: Lithuania catapult flight cover. Additional franking on back to make up 8.50 Litas rate.

The supplementary flight service to the ships at sea was continued until August 1939. The catapult service, however, was ended.

The German North Atlantic catapult airmails were a significant step in the advancement of transatlantic mail. In spite of the fact that much of the catapult airmail was philatelically inspired, it is a rich area for the aeropostal historian and researcher, particularly in foreign rates.

Bibliography:

"Brückenpfeiler auf dem Nordatlantik", Lufthansa Nachrichten, No 169, 1959.
Van Beveren, Frans J. 1982. *De Ontwikkeling Van De Trans-Atlantische Luchtpostverbindinge*. Heeze, Netherlands.
Davies, R.E.G. 1991. *Lufthansa: An Airline and Its Aircraft*. New York, New York: Orion Books.

DuFour, Jacques. 1963. *Catalogue des Liaisons transatlantiques par Hydravions catapultes*. Bruxelles, Belgium: Editions De La Revue Postale.

Graue, James W. "German Catapult Airmail in the North Atlantic, 1925-1935." *German Postal Specialist*. Vol 19 (February 1968) no 2: 53-60.

Haberer, Erich. 1985. *Katalog über die Katapultpost, Teil 1: Nordatlantik*. Published by the author: Weil der Stadt, Germany.

Heinkel, Ernst. 1956. *Stormy Life*. E. P. Dutton: New York. English translation.

Kayssner, Kurt. 1933. *Deutscher Schleuderflugpost Katalog (Catalogue of German Catapult Flights)*. Bad Buckow, Germany. First Issue, Bilingual German - English.

-----. 1934. *Grosser Deutscher Schleuderflugpost Katalog*. Bad Buckow, Germany.

-----. 1935. *Schleuderflugpost Katalog und Handbuch*, Bad Buckow, Germany.

-----. 1936. *Schleuderflugpost Katalog und Handbuch, Nachtrag*. Supplement 1936. Bad Buckow, Germany.

Kohl, Roland et al. 1984. *Schweizerisches Luftpost-Handbuch*. Hinwil, Switzerland: Schweizerischer Aerophilatelisten-Verein.

Stanley-Smith, Roger G. 1990. *The North Atlantic Catapult, Part 1 and Part 2*. Hurstpierpoint, West Sussex, Great Britain.

Schmidt, Hermann: "Schleuderflüge von Bord der Dampfer *"Bremen"* und *"Europa," Postgeschichtliche Blätter aus dem Weser-Ems-Gebiet"* (Postal history reports from the Weser-Ems area) Vol 1 (June 1959) no 13.

"Die Katapult-und Schleuderflüge." *Deutsche Zeitung für Briefmarkenkunde*. December 20, 1965.

James W. Graue is editor of the *Airpost Journal*. He is an active aerophilatelic author, exhibitor and a national judge. His areas of interest include all German transatlantic airmails, the 1934 airmail issues of Germany, and the Third Reich area. In addition to the American Air Mail Society, he is active in the Northwest Federation of Stamp Clubs and the Germany Philatelic Society.

9

The Lindbergh Circle

by George Sioras

A surprisingly obscure aerophilatelic event took place in February 1931. Souvenir airmail covers such as the one shown in Figure 1 announced the "Completing of the Lindbergh Circle," the development of Foreign Air Mail (FAM) Routes 5 and 6.

This completing of the circle was not obscure to the airmail fraternity. The flights that achieved this milestone had been announced in the *United States Official Postal Bulletin,* airmail collectors and dealers had taken note, and many souvenir covers were serviced. And the aerophilatelic press took note. The *Airpost Journal* ran a report on this event. Since two foreign airmail routes were involved, The *Air Mail Collector* provided two reports, one on FAM 5, the other on FAM 6.

The flights are also recorded in the *American Air Mail Catalogue* under FAM Routes 5 and 6. Interestingly, in the 1931 reports on the completion of the Lindbergh Circle, there is neither any mention of Lindbergh himself nor any discussion of the circle. The aerophilatelic literature assumed that the Lindbergh Circle was a familiar topic to all airmail collectors; all that was necessary was to record details on the flights.

And the rest of the world did not seem to care. In the late 1920s and the early 1930s, aviation events were of high interest, often front page news. And anything related to Lindbergh was of extraordinarily high interest, typically front page news and frequently with very big headlines. So it comes as a surprise to find that this occasion yielded no headlines. In fact, there seem to have been no news reports at all.

Nevertheless, there is a story behind this obscure, non-newsworthy event. And while some parts of the story are familiar, others apparently have not been recorded in the aerophilatelic literature. So we will review the story here, touching lightly on episodes familiar to the airmail fraternity and providing information to fill blanks where we can.

As noted in the Lindbergh section of the *American Air Mail Catalogue,* the Lindbergh Circle has its roots in the Latin American Goodwill Tour (LAGWT). But at this point there is a substantial information gap, and there is no explanation available regarding the origins of the LAGWT.

Since the United States Goodwill Tour (USGWT) had been completed a few weeks earlier, it is tempting to think that the LAGWT just naturally followed the USGWT and was pretty much the same thing. But that was not the case at all. The USGWT was a well-organized and extensively publicized activity. It was jointly sponsored by the Guggenheim Fund for the Promotion of Aeronautics and the United States Department of Commerce. Careful planning provided that there would be at least one stop in each of the then forty-eight states. And a detailed itinerary with schedule times for the entire three months was available before the tour started. This is in sharp contrast to the LAGWT for which there were no sponsors, no advanced planning, and no established itinerary.

It is more or less common knowledge, at least in specialized Lindbergh circles, that Lindbergh was invited to visit Mexico City, the first stop on the LAGWT, and that the invitation was arranged by Dwight Morrow, United States Ambassador to Mexico. But, when we look for an explanation of how the visit to Mexico City developed into a tour of twenty-one nations, we find very little that is helpful, either in the aerophilatelic literature or in the various Lindbergh biographies.

If we were to ask a related question—why did the Ambassador of the United States want Lindbergh to visit Mexico City—we would find that the real beginning of the Lindbergh Circle lies in Paris, in the days following the non-stop flight from New York. On completion of the flight to Paris, Lindbergh became the honored guest of the United States Ambassador to France, Myron C. Herrick. At the time, Ambassador Herrick had a problem. Diplomatic relations between the United States and France had not been going well. But soon after Lindbergh dropped in on him, literally out of the sky, things changed.

Here are Herrick's own words (from Bentley T. Mott: *Myron T. Herrick, Friend of France*):

"At the very moment Lindbergh started from America, we were in one of those periods of petulant nagging and quarreling between the French and ourselves which have flared up and died down more than once since the Armistice. I have lived through enough of these nasty equinoctial storms not to let them worry me very much, for not all the newspapers on both sides of the Atlantic can ever seriously affect the solid basis of our mutual feelings. But I hate this bad weather and like to see it clear up.

Within ten hours after Lindbergh landed at Le Bourget all the clouds were rolling away, and in another twenty-four the sun was shining brightly."

Figure 1: "Completing the Lindbergh Circle." Cover flown from Miami, postmarked February 9, 1931, to Maturin, backstamped February 11, 1931.

Morrow, of course, knew about Lindbergh's stay in Paris, and his visits to Brussels and London. He was very much aware of the strong positive impact that such goodwill events can have on diplomatic relations. And Morrow had serious diplomatic problems in Mexico. In 1916, there had been a very nasty incident when Pancho Villa raided a small United States town across the border. In retaliation the United States sent an expeditionary force (an invading army) into Mexico. Bad feelings that had existed since the Mexican-American War were exacerbated.

Additional causes of tension developed after the United States entered World War I, including a proposed alliance between Mexico and Germany. In the aftermath the gringos found themselves very much disliked in Mexico. The diplomatic prospects facing Morrow when he was appointed to be Ambassador to Mexico in 1927 were not promising. And he wondered. If Lindbergh were to drop in on Mexico City, might the diplomatic clouds roll away as they had in Paris?

So he arranged with the President of Mexico to issue a formal invitation asking Lindbergh to come to Mexico City. And once again, the stormy weather immediately rolled away and the diplomatic sun shone brightly.

It is at this point that we come up against the substantial information gap mentioned above. As noted, the aerophilatelic literature does not provide any information on how the rest of the LAGWT happened. Nor are explanations provided in the various Lindbergh biographies. Lindbergh wrote a long article, "To Bogota and Back by Air," for the *National Geographic Magazine*. One might expect to find something there on how the tour may have developed. But the only related statement, not very helpful, is found at the beginning of the account:

"I always had a desire to fly in the tropics; also, I was particularly interested in the feasibility of Pan American airlines; consequently, when I received an invitation from the President of Mexico to visit his country, it required less than a week to complete my preparation for the flight."

To develop information on how the tour was extended, newspaper microfilms from 1927 were examined. The notes that follow suggest how and when the rest of the tour fell into place:

1927,

Dec 8   Lindbergh announces Mexico City flight. Personal invitation from President Calles. "No official connection."

Dec 10   Formal invitation from General Machado, President of Cuba, to fly from Mexico City to Havana. Can not act on invitation at this time.

Dec 14   Arrives in Mexico City.

Dec 15   Accepts invitation to go to Panama.

Dec 16   Will visit Central American countries. Tentative route: El Salvador, Guatemala, Honduras, Panama, then return to Mexico on way to Havana.

Dec 18   Reported that he will meet President Coolidge at Pan-American Congress in Havana.

Dec 28   Will circle rest of Caribbean; unexpected announcement of continuation of flight made just before leaving Mexico City.

The assertion that the visit to Mexico had no official connection appears to have been a diplomatic pleasantry. The news reports provide strong indications of considerable official action. While in Mexico City, Charles Lindbergh stayed at the United States Embassy. Apparently there were exchanges of cables between the Embassy in Mexico City and the State Department in Washington preceding each announcement of a change in Lindbergh's plans.

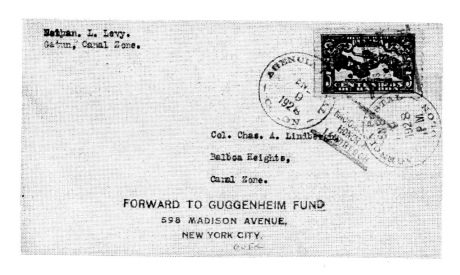

Figure 2: First Day Cover of 5-cent Panama Lindbergh stamp with 3-line "Forward to Guggenheim Fund" rubber stamp cachet. Front and back of cover are shown.

The unsubstantiated assertion found in one source, that the LAGWT was sponsored by the State Department, seems to have been close to the mark. While "sponsored by" may be a bit of an overstatement, it appears very clear that the State Department was substantially involved and that the LAGWT was arranged with the complete cooperation of United States diplomatic personnel.

With a little Kentucky windage applied to the news reports, the following sequence of events emerges. When it was announced that Lindbergh would be going to Mexico City, he was invited to Havana. Although no immediate action was taken on the invitation to Cuba, Lindbergh must have decided early on that he would go to Havana for the Pan-American Congress, scheduled for January 16 through February 20, 1928.

At about the time Lindbergh arrived in Mexico City, an invitation to come to Panama was received. This was shortly followed by invitations from several other Central American countries.

When it was announced that Lindbergh would be going to Central America, invitations from South American countries resulted. Since the decision had been made to go to Havana for the Pan-American Congress, and since time permitted, it was then decided that a complete circuit of the Caribbean would be made. And, as noted, Ambassador Morrow and the embassy staff in Mexico City were extensively involved in making the necessary arrangements — unofficially, of course.

Figure 2 is an interesting commemorative cover, which also happens to be an unusual First Day Cover. It was postmarked in Colon, at the beginning of Lindbergh's visit to Panama and the Canal Zone. The three-line rubber stamped cachet indicates that the Guggenheim Fund, which sponsored the USGWT, may have been involved with the LAGWT.

No evidence has been found to shed additional light on this matter. The cover is shown to suggest that, conceivably, there could be further developments in this part of the story.

On the last stop of the LAGWT, Lindbergh found Pan American Airways operating FAM 4 between Key West and Havana. This was the first step in the to-be-developed Lindbergh Circle.

The interesting map shown in Figure 3, accompanies a long newspaper article by Richard F. Hoyt, Chairman of the Board of Pan American Airways. The article discusses Pan American's plans for developing this Lindbergh Circle, even though the name, Lindbergh Circle, apparently had not come into use at that time. The two following paragraphs from Hoyt's article are of particular interest:

"It is significant to note that a portion of this system encircles the Caribbean Sea over almost identically the route flown by Col. Charles A. Lindbergh in his famous goodwill tour. He also prepared these peoples for this aviation development.

He arrived in Havana, it may be recalled, and piloted a Pan American Airways transport in a series of trips over the harbor, carrying as passengers delegates to the Pan-American Congress."

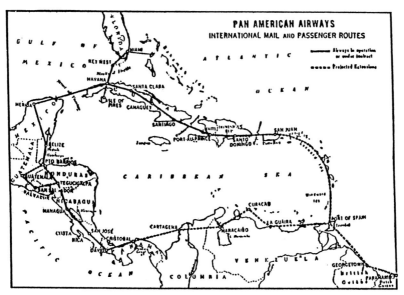

Figure 3: Map depicting scheduled PAA routes around the Caribbean, later known as The Lindbergh Circle, San Francisco Examiner, December 23, 1928.

After FAM Route No 4, the next step in the development of the Lindbergh Circle was taken on January 9, 1929, when FAM 6 began operations between Miami and San Juan, Puerto Rico. Two days later, it was announced that Lindbergh was to become the technical advisor to Pan American Airways and would pilot the FAM Route No 5 inaugural flight to the Panama Canal Zone. On February 2, 1929, during pre-inaugural festivities, we find Lindbergh again flying people around in a Pan Am airplane, this time over Miami.

When the FAM 5 inaugural took place, many photographs were taken as usual, including aerial photographs of Lindbergh's arrival in the Canal Zone. One was used to make the illustrated post card, shown in Figure 4.

Figure 4: Aerial photo postcard of arrival at Panama on completion of FAM 5 inaugural southbound, carried on the inaugural northbound flight with the 26-cent post card rate.

The card shows Lindbergh's plane approaching the Canal Zone on the south-bound leg. The post card was flown back to the United States on the northbound leg. This post card is a particularly interesting souvenir of this flight because it illustrates the unusual 26-cent airmail rate which applied to post cards. From this point on, the development of FAM 5 and 6, which constituted the Lindbergh Circle, is well-documented in the *American Air Mail Catalogue*.

We will finish with another interesting cover commemorating the completion of the circle with a printed cachet in Spanish (Figure 5). A significant part of the interest stems from the fact that the printing on this cover includes the address of the Berkshire Exchange, which published the first seventeen issues of The *Airpost Journal*, and then turned the monthly magazine over to the American Air Mail Society whose official society publication it has been since October 1931.

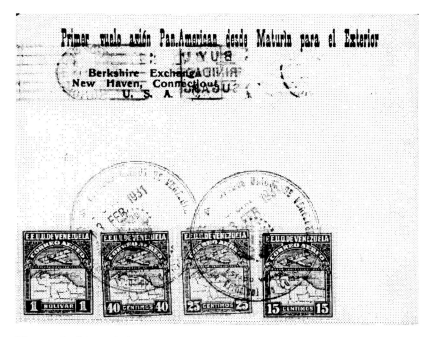

Figure 5: "Completing the Lindbergh Circle." Cover flown from Maturin, Venezuela (postmarked February 13, 1931) to Port-of-Spain, Trinidad (back-stamped February 13, 1931), showing unusual printed cachet in Spanish.

One Last Comment

It is a curious circumstance that, although the duration of Lindbergh's LAGWT visit to Mexico lasted two weeks, from December 14 through 28, 1927, aerophilatelic souvenirs from that occasion appear to be extraordinarily scarce. There do not seem to be any covers that have been illustrated in the aerophilatelic literature, none of the major Lindbergh exhibits are known to have any, and none have turned up in the inspection of many thousands of airmail covers. The *American Air Mail Catalogue* has listed Mexico City covers since the Lindbergh section was first published in 1940 but they all seem to have disappeared.

Bibliography:

The Air Mail Collector, "Completing the Lindbergh Circle, FAM 5-6, Feb. 12, 1931." Vol 3 (May 1931) no 7: 17.
The Air Mail Collector. "Completing the Lindbergh Circle, FAM 5-6, Feb. 11, 1931." Vol 3 (June 1931) no 8: 12.
The Airpost Journal, "*F.A.M. 5-6 Extension.*" Vol 2 (March 1931) no 4: 5.
Blumenthal, Frank et al. 1981. "Completing 'The Lindbergh Circle'- Extension to Maturin, Venezuela, and Port of Spain, Trinidad, February 10, 1931." "Foreign Contract Air Mail Routes (FAM's)." *American Air Mail Catalogue*. Vol 4 ed 5: 1766-1767. Cinnaminson, New Jersey: American Air Mail Society.
Hoyt, Richard F. "Plane lines soon to link two America." *The San Francisco Examiner*, December 23, 1928: 6.
Kleinert, Florence and George K. Sioras. 1978. "Lindberghiana." *American Air Mail Catalogue*. Vol 3 ed 5: 1438-1478. Cinnaminson, New Jersey: American Air Mail Society.
Lindbergh, Colonel. Charles A., "To Bogota and Back," *National Geographic Magazine*, Vol 53 (May 1928) no 5: 529-601.
Mott, T. Bentley. 1929. *Myron T. Herrick, Friend of France*. Garden City, NY: Doubleday, Doran & Company.

George K. Sioras edits the combined newsletters for the Lindbergh Collectors Club and the Metropolitan Air Mail Society. His collecting interests include Lindbergh, Pacific and Atlantic airmail to 1945, New England aerophilately, airships, early CAMs and airmail rates on cover. He is a member of the American Air Mail Society, Aerophilatelic Federation of the Americas, the Philatelic Group of Boston, and the Cardinal Spellman Philatelic Museum.

10

Mermoz

Trans-Atlantic

Flights, 1930

by E. P. Sloan

The year 1930 was an eventful year in the history of South Atlantic air-mail development.

In March, the Germans had established the experimental combined sea and air service with the planes of the Deutsche Lufthansa and the Condor Syndicate, meeting the ships *Cap Arcona* and *Cap Polonio* of the Hamburg Süd Amerika Steamship Line to speed up the delivery of mail to and from South America.

In May, Jean Mermoz made the first commercial mail flight across the South Atlantic for Aéropostale.

Also in May, the *Graf Zeppelin* carried mail to South America on its Pan American flight.

Finally, in December, the mass flight by the Italian Squadron, under the command of General Italo Balbo, from Rome to Rio de Janeiro was successfully completed.

This article describes the flights across the South Atlantic Ocean, carried out by Jean Mermoz for the Compagnie Général Aéropostale (CGA or Aéropostale) in May and July 1930.

Early in 1930, Aéropostale had reached a critical stage in its development. The line from Toulouse, France, to Dakar in Senegal, was well established and operating efficiently.

In South America great strides were made in expanding the network. Regularly scheduled weekly services between Buenos Aires and Natal and Rio de Janeiro connected with the Aéropostale mail ships (Aviso) which carried the mail to and from Dakar. Buenos Aires was linked to the south with the cities and oil fields of Patagonia, to the west with Mendoza and Santiago, Chile; and to the north with Asunción, capital of Paraguay.

The only link in this vast network which remained to be conquered by aircraft was the South Atlantic gap between Dakar and Natal, Brazil.

Jean Mermoz

By 1930, Jean Mermoz was a veteran airline pilot, with many achievements to his credit. He had joined the company, then Latécoère, in 1924 and had flown mail through Spain to Morocco.

In 1926, while flying the Casablanca—Dakar route, he had been captured and held for ransom by a rebel band in Spanish Sahara.

In late 1927, Mermoz was transferred to Buenos Aires, Argentina, and made Chief Pilot of Aéropostale in South America. On December 7, 1927, he made his first mail flight between Buenos Aires and Rio de Janeiro.

On March 1, 1928, he flew the first Argentine mail from Europe to Rio from where it was flown to Natal to meet the CGA Aviso *Péronne* which carried it to Dakar.

On April 16, 1928, he introduced night flying by making the first night flight between Rio and Buenos Aires. Night flying later became the standard practice throughout the line and reduced the mail transit time significantly by eliminating the overnight stops.

In November 1928, Mermoz made the first of several survey flights between Buenos Aires and Santiago, Chile.

In 1929, he made two forced landings in the Andes from which he and his companions made heroic escapes. Mermoz also carried out survey flights from Buenos Aires to Patagonia in Southern Argentina and to Asunción in Paraguay. He was also the first to fly over the jungles of southern Brazil directly from Rio De Janeiro to Bolivia.

When he was recalled from duty in South America in February 1930, Mermoz was famous throughout South America, but little known in France. He was the obvious choice to attempt the first mail flight across the South Atlantic for Aéropostale.

The Aircraft

Mermoz was recalled to France to conduct trial flights with a Latécoère 28 aircraft, a land plane which had been fitted with floats. This modification was necessary to meet the requirements of the French Government that "only a Hydroavion could be used to attempt the trans-Atlantic crossing." The Laté 28 was designed to carry 660 pounds of mail and eight passengers. It was equipped with a single 600 horsepower Hispano-Suiza liquid cooled engine, had a cruising speed of 125 miles per hour, and a range of about 2,000 miles. This modified version was known as Latécoère 28-3, and Mermoz christened the aircraft *Comte de la Vaulx,* in honor of the President of the International Aero-nautical Federation, his friend and flying companion who had been killed in an aircraft crash in the United States in 1929. The Laté 28-3 has been commemorated by stamps issued in several countries. Figure 1 shows the one issued in 1964 by Monaco (Scott No.578).

Figure 1: Monaco stamp shows Laté 28-3 *Comte de la Vaulx.*

At the end of March, Mermoz began training on hydroplanes, which he had never flown, and in ten days he qualified for his commercial license.

On April 11 and 12, 1930, Mermoz, set a new world record for time and distance in the modified Laté 28, covering a distance of 2,650 miles in a flight which lasted 30 hours and 25 minutes on a closed circuit course at

Marignane. This established the capability of the aircraft to fly the 1,800+ miles between Africa and South America. Plans were completed for an early attempt at the crossing.

On this record flight, Mermoz was accompanied by Jean Dabry, navigator, and Leonard Gimié as radio operator.

The Westward Flight

Mermoz was determined that Aéropostale should be the first to make a commercial mail flight across the South Atlantic. He was aware that, in Germany, preparations were well underway for the flight of the *Graf Zeppelin* to South and North America.

May 12, when the moon would be full, was selected as a target date, and on that date everything was in readiness. The Laté 28-3 was in Saint Louis, Senegal, tuned up, with a full load of fuel.

When the 275 pounds of mail which had left Toulouse twenty-five hours earlier, arrived and was loaded aboard the aircraft, Mermoz with Dabry and Gimié took off and set course for Brazil at 11:00 A.M. on May 12. Some 20 hours later, after flying through an intense tropical storm and enduring severe heat and humidity, they landed at Natal.

The mail was immediately turned over to Vanier who carried it to Rio de Janeiro. From Rio it was flown to Buenos Aires by Reine, and from Buenos Aires to Santiago, Chile by Henri Guillaumet. Mail which had left Toulouse on May 11, was delivered in Brazil in two days, in Argentina in three days, and in Chile in four days.

The mail carried on this first flight included regular commercial mail, specially cacheted mail from Paris, and mail picked up at various points along the Aéropostale route.

Figure 2 shows a commercial cover mailed in London on May 8 and backstamped in Rio on May 13.

Figure 3 is a letter with a special cachet mailed in Paris on May 10 and backstamped in Buenos Aires on May 14, 1930. This cover is also signed by Dabry. Although there was a total of 275 pounds of mail carried, only six covers were recorded from Senegal.

Figure 2: Commercial flown cover flown by Jean Mermoz. Posted in England on May 8, backstamped in Rio de Janeiro, Brazil, on May 13, 1930.

Figure 3: Cover posted in Paris on May 10, backstamped Buenos Aires, on May 14, 1930. Special cachet and signature by Dabry, navigator.

Figure 4: Cover posted in Saint Louis, Senegal on May 12. Backstamped in Natal, Brazil on May 13, 1930. Special cachet and signature of Mermoz.

Figure 4 shows a cover, signed by Mermoz and with a special cachet for the flight, which was mailed in Saint Louis, Senegal, on May 12 and backstamped in Natal on May 13, 1930.

The Return Flight

After his successful westward crossing of the Atlantic, Mermoz planned to make the return flight on June 8. Mail for this flight was accepted by all of the South American countries served by Aéropostale, and special cachets were applied. A total of 320 pounds of such mail had arrived in Natal for the planned departure.

However, Mermoz was unable to get the fully loaded Laté 28-3 to take off from the waters of the Rio Potingi at Natal.

Figure 5: Cover prepared for the return flight and signed by Mermoz. Crossed the Atlantic by Aviso ship. Mailed in Buenos Aires on June 6, 1930; backstamped in Paris on June 18, 1930.

Figure 6: Cover prepared for return flight but sent by sea mail. Posted in Asunción, Paraguay on June 6 and backstamped in England on June 19, 1930.

By June 12, he had made thirty-five take-off attempts without success. At this point he decided that the mail could not be delayed any longer and it was dispatched by the regular Aviso service of CGA. This mail, which left Natal on June 12, arrived in Paris and was backstamped on or about June 18, 1930. These covers are usually described in the French literature as *"Premier essai"* (First attempt).

Figure 5 shows a cover signed by Mermoz, with the Argentine cachet for the flight, which was sent by sea. It was backstamped in Paris on June 18, 1930.

Figure 6 shows a similar cover from Paraguay with the large circular cachet. It, too, went by Aviso ship and was backstamped in England on June 19, 1930.

After sending the mail by ship on June 12, Mermoz decided that the prevailing winds and water conditions on the Rio Potingi at Natal were not satisfactory, and that a new take off site must be found.

After a survey flight around the area, he decided on the Bay of Bonfim, about 40 miles north of Natal. After further delays for modifications to the aircraft structure and waiting for full moon conditions, attempts to get the aircraft into the air commenced again in early July. Finally, on the afternoon of July 8, on the fifty-third attempt, Mermoz was successful and headed for Dakar.

However, his troubles were not yet over. About 550 miles west of Dakar, an oil line ruptured and Mermoz had to make an emergency landing on the open sea. He landed alongside the steamship *Phocee* with which the aircraft had been in radio contact. Mermoz, the crew, and the mail were taken aboard the ship. A tow-line was attached to the aircraft but the plane keeled over and sank.

The mail was carried by the ship to Dakar and flown from there to Paris where it arrived and was backstamped on July 16, 1930. These covers are only identifiable by the date of the backstamp. No cachet or other indication of the crash was used. These covers are usually described as *"deuxième essai"* (second attempt) in the French literature.

Figure 7 shows another crash cover. It was mailed in Montevideo on July 4 and bears the Uruguay cachet for the Mermoz flight with the addition of the date stamp for July 5, 1930. The cover is backstamped in Paris on July 16, 1930.

Figure 7: Flown on return flight from Natal to Dakar by Mermoz, posted in Montevideo and addressed to Paris.

Conclusion

These 1930 flights by Mermoz and his companions served a number of purposes.

These flights demonstrated that regular airmail flights across the South Atlantic were possible. They also, however, proved the need for better equipment and resulted in Aéropostale placing orders for long range multi-engine flying boats for the South Atlantic crossing.

Unfortunately, these new aircraft did not begin to appear until 1933 and regular weekly all air service did not commence on the line until 1936.

Finally, Mermoz set new records, not only in making the two way crossing of the Atlantic, but in dogged determination and singleness of purpose. No other pilot, before or since, has equaled his efforts in making fifty-three attempts to get his aircraft airborne. Covers carried on these flights are treasured by airmail collectors as mementoes of a most significant event in the history of aviation and in the history of trans-Atlantic airmail service.

Bibliography:

Kronstein, Dr. Max et al. 1974. "Early foreign flights, commonly called foreign pioneer flights." *American Air Mail Catalogue*, Vol 1 ed 5: 201. Washington, DC: Ameri-can Air Mail Society.

Lüning, Orjan et al. 1981. "Trans-Oceanic Record Flights.". *American Air Mail Catalogue*. Vol 4 ed 5: 1556-1557. Cinnaminson, New Jersey: American Air Mail Society.

Collot, Gérard and Alain Cornu. 1990. *Ligne Mermoz, Histoire Aérophilate-lique, Latécoère, Aéropostale, Air France, 1918-1940*, Paris, France: Editions Bertrand Sinais.

Davies, R.E.G. 1984. *Airlines of Latin America since 1919*. London, England: Smithsonian Insti-ution Press, Putnam.

Fleury, Jean-Gérard F. 1974. *L'Atlantique Sud de l'Aéropostale á Concorde*. Paris, France: Editions Denoël

Fleury, Jean-Gérard F. 1949. *La Ligne Mermoz*. Gallimard: Paris.

Kessel, Joseph. 1938. *Mermoz*. Paris, France: Gallimard.

Mermoz, Jean. 1951. *Mes Vols*. Paris, France: Flammarion.

Dumont-Fouya, A. "1961. La Ligne Mermoz." Paris, France: Cercle Aérophi-latélique Français.

Emmett Patrick Sloan is President of the Canadian Aerophilatelic Society. He collects and exhibits nationally and internationally the development of commercial services between Europe and South America before World War II that established the South Atlantic airmail service. His society memberships include the American Air Mail Society, American Philatelic Society, Royal Philatelic Society of Canada, Cercle Aerophila-télique Français, and other international airmail organizations.

11

The Chicago 1933 Gordon Bennett Cup Race

by **Erich Schröder**
and
Stephen Neulander

The Gordon Bennett Balloon Cup (and Airplane) Races were started in large part to promote the newspaper, the *New York Herald*, which was owned by the man for whom the races were named. During the late 1890s and the early part of the 20th century, newspaper competition was fierce. The city of New York had more than twenty daily publications. The need to do something unusual to promote the circulation, something that was exclusive, was essential.

Thus James Gordon Bennett recognized that he, too, needed to do something to stimulate the circulation of his paper. It was also important to his overseas paper—The *Herald-Tribune International* as well. The Gordon Bennett Cup Races were part of this effort.

The *New York Herald* was founded in 1835 by Bennett's father and was taken over by him in 1872. James Gordon Bennett's reputation as a New York socialite, gambler, and playboy had already been started.

His wealth and position allowed him to become involved in sporting events. And this sporting involvement lead him eventually to sponsor the great balloon races.

J. Gordon Bennett became part of a syndicate betting with other members of the exclusive Union Club that they would win a cross-Atlantic race. This race from New Jersey to the Isle of Wight in Great Britain was won. The prize of $90,000 was set aside to later became the start-up fund that enabled him to underwrite the Gordon Bennett Race Cups and other events.

Bennett was enthusiastic about many different sports activities. It is reported that he introduced the games of polo and lawn tennis to the New York City Society, and thus to the United States. Although considered a bit eccentric, he was accepted in upper society due to his position and wealth. Upper society tolerated most of his extravagances, up to a duel which he provoked. After that, many formerly open doors were shut to him. At the close of the 1890s, he moved his residence to Paris. There, he continued his life style for the next forty-two years, in a large mansion with many servants, as well as more than twenty dogs, cats and several parakeets. One bird supposedly greeted him every morning with a cheerful "Good Morning, Commodore!" Around the turn of the century, he purchased the largest motor-yacht of the world and discovered speed. This new love prompted donations of trophies and cups for automobile, airplane, and speed boat races.

James Gordon Bennett also gave rise to headlines for his newspaper by financing expeditions to different areas of the world. The search for the African explorer Dr. David Livingstone by Henry Stanley was initiated by Bennett. A lake in Alaska, a mountain peak and river in Algeria, and an island in Siberia are just a few sites which still bear his name reminding us of a man and his life during which he is reported to have spent about $40 million.

At first Bennett sponsored the *Coupe Internationale d'Automobile*, but when officials balked at his rules for the 1906 race and refused to accept them, he decided to establish an international balloon prize. This, he determined, would continue to establish him as a philanthropist of sport.

The rules of the *Coupe Internationale des Aéronautique* were simple and straightforward. It was not to be a race, but rather a distance contest.

The Gordon Bennett competition was opened to free balloons ranging in size from 22,000 to 80,000 cubic feet in capacity. Entries were to be chosen by the national clubs belonging to the Fédération Aéronautique Internationale (FAI).

Figure 1: Caricature card prepared for James Gordon Bennett, postmarked at Heathrow airport, London.

The trophy was to be retained by the first country that successfully won the competition three times in a row. The winning country was to be the host of the next year's competition. A $2,500 cash prize was to be awarded to the winning crew during the first three years of the competition and then abandoned, once the event was permanently established.

Because of the rules, there were actually three James Gordon Bennett trophies. Belgium retired the first in 1924, the United States captured the second in 1928, and the third cup remained in competition until the final event prior to World War II.

The first Gordon Bennett classic attracted sixteen balloons from seven countries. This included Alberto Santos-Dumont, who entered under the colors of the Aero Club of America, flying his airship *Deux Amériques*. This was the first and only time a powered vehicle was to participate in a Gordon Bennett Balloon Race.

The first Bennett Race, flown from the center of Paris on September 9, 1906, was won by Lieutenant Frank P. Lahm of the United States. It established the oldest international air competition, one that continues to this day. The basic rules that were set in 1906 are still intact. The country that wins the trophy consecutively three times gets to retire it.

In the next eighty years, the race was hosted not only by the United States and France, but also by Poland, Switzerland, Austria, and Germany.

All eyes turned to Chicago, Illinois, in 1933. The Century of Progress Exhibition was being held and the "City of Clout" used every bit it had to gather the National Balloon Competition (which qualified the balloons that were to take part in the Gordon Bennett), the Gordon Bennett Cup Race and the National Air Races (for airplanes).

The race took place on September 2, 1933. It was partially sponsored by the *Chicago Daily News* which not only donated the new trophy Cup, but also offered a prize of $2,000 to the winner. In the years of depression spreading around the world, this was a sizeable sum.

An estimated crowd of 80,000 spectators watched the balloons take off from Curtiss-Wright Field in Glenview, Illinois. The German balloon *OPEL*, which was to be flown by the rocket experimenter Fritz von Opel, broke away from the ropes restraining it prior to take off and was destroyed The skin from the balloon provided excellent souvenirs, especi-ally when autographed by Fritz von Opel.

The rest of the field managed to take-off in a normal fashion.

Now it was up to the pilots and the balloons to see who would win the competition.The following balloons participated:

Participants of the 1933 Chicago Gordon Bennett Balloon Race

U.S.A.	*U.S.Navy*	Lieutenant T.G.W. "Tex" Settle Lieutenant Charles A. Kendall
U.S.A.	*Goodyear IX*	Ward T. van Orman Frank A. Trotter
Belgium		Philippe Quersin Marcel van Schelle
France	*Verdun*	Georges Ravaine Georges M. Blanchet
Poland	*Kosciuszko*	Francyzek Hynek Lieutenant Zbigniew Burzynski
Germany	*Deutschland*	Richard Schütze Dr. Erich Körner

Figure 2: Three cachets were used during the event. The top cover was posted at the Railway Postal Car Exhibition, Chicago, Illinois, while the bottom cover was posted in Glenview. It shows the signature of van Orman who took third place.

Due to their design and construction, the balloons from Belgium and the Netherlands landed on the eastern shores of Michigan, fearing that they might not be able to cross Lake Huron and in the dark of the night would crash into it. The chances of rescue would be dim. The French balloon, drifted in another direction because of a lower altitude of flight and came down in northern Ohio after staying aloft long enough to cover only 154.38 miles.

Lieutenant Commander T.G.W."Tex" Settle, winner of the 1932 race, led the American contingent in the 1933 competition. Ward T. van Orman, who had won the race for America on other occasions, was a reluctant entry. Settle and his aid, Lieutenant C.H. Kendall, brought their balloon, *U.S. Navy,* down near Branford, Connecticut, after a relatively uneventful flight covering 750 miles. This turned out to be good for second place.

The other two balloons had a great deal more trouble. Van Orman did not want to fly at first. His wife had passed away the year prior and he was left to raise three small children. However, Paul Litchfield of Goodyear wanted an entry in the race and van Orman was his pilot. When Litchfield consented to insure van Orman for the children's security, van Orman agreed to enter the race. Studying the weather reports just before reaching the Great Lakes, he scheduled his trip over the Great Lakes with a landing spot in Newfoundland. A potential dunking in Lake Michigan altered that plan, but he and his co-pilot, Frank Trotter, crossed safely into Canada, only then to be caught in a thunderstorm.

As van Orman later wrote:

> "The most notable thing at first was darkness. We were flying at 8,000 feet, yet everything was black as ink. It got worse and worse. Suddenly the squall came with a roaring rush. When it struck, we had never seen a balloon act as ours acted — not even in the Pittsburgh storm. It hit us while we were high and we careened all over, bounced all over. We rushed up and fell and we were only on the outskirts of it! Had we been in the center of that disturbance, I'm certain we would have been dead at the start."

Even though they had parachutes on board, the pilots would have been unable to jump due to gale-like winds, so they fought it out for more than six hours. The balloon, *Goodyear IX,* finally crashed to the ground through a forest of tree tops, smashing into five trees and having the envelope torn apart by a sixth. There, twenty-five feet above ground, the men hung until daylight.

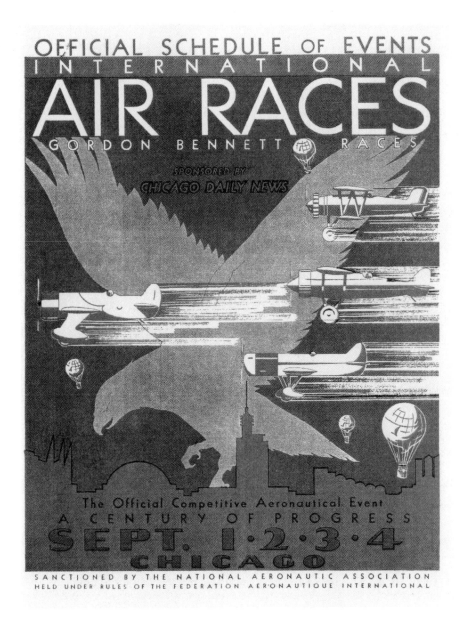

Figure 3: Poster for the 1933 Gordon Bennett Cup Race, Chicago, Illinois.

It took fourteen days of hiking through the forest wilderness in fierce rains to reach anything resembling civilization, and that was a railroad line shack. By cutting the telephone line, the two were able to attract enough attention to be rescued. Van Orman and Trotter stayed alive by shooting grouse with a rifle found in the cabin.

At the same time the wilderness of Canada and the northern part of the United States was searched for another balloon crew, the Polish balloon. The *Kosciuszko* had flown a distance of 846 miles in a flying time of 38 hours, 32 minutes, and landed near Quebec in Canada, taking the first place. Francyzek Hynek and Lieutenant Zbigniew Burzynski had to travel even further than van Orman and Trotter to be rescued, ninety miles.

With these rescues, the Gordon Bennett Race of 1933 came to an end.

Several aerophilatelic souvenir covers are known from this event. Some were postmarked at the Chicago World's Fair or directly at the airfield. It appears that some covers were postmarked at two other sites, one at the northern boundary of Chicago, and the second at Glenview. The same cachets were applied either in black, red, or blue. A red and blue vignette was also frequently used on souvenir mail. On-board mail is known to have been carried by all participating balloons.

Demonstration flights of all sorts completed the aviation program. But there were other memorable events. One of the more famous aviators at that meet was the German pilot Major Ernst Udet. Professor Jean Piccard was also a guests of honor. His balloon capsule was on exhibition. It was this capsule which was used later that year by Settle to set a altitude record. It was also used by Jean and Jeanette Piccard when she became the first woman to go into the stratosphere. Another favorite with the visitors was a tethered balloon where one could experience a balloon ride for $1.10.

Conclusion

It might be of interest to list the results of the Gordon Bennett Balloon Race of the following years: a Polish team won in Warsaw, Poland, in 1934 and 1935. Ernest Demuyter from Belgium took the first place in 1936 and 1937, and in 1938, Poland became the winner again.

Due to the disruptions of World War II and the bad economy in the years to follow, the race did not start again until 1983. The first postwar race was held at Paris. France, Poland, Switzerland, and Austria have been recent victors.

Figure 4: On-board mail was carried by almost every balloon which was then posted at the landing site. Shown is a cover flown and signed by United States pilot, T.G.W. Settle.

Figure 5: A red and blue cachet was imprinted on envelopes, the cover shown was posted at the Exhibition Station.

Overall, the Gordon Bennett Balloon Races are a fertile field for aerophilatelists and collectors. Since they ran continuously from the end of World War I to 1938, and again from 1983 to date (to say nothing of 1906 through 1914), there are many items to be sought for the complete history to be compiled. The search, and the stories that go with the pieces found, make it rewarding to the historian and the aerophilatelist.

Bibliography:

Burzynski, Kpt. Obs. Bal. Zbigniew. 1934. *Kosciuszko nad Ameryka*. Aeroklub Warschau.
Crouch, Thomas D. 1983. *The Eagle Aloft*. Smithsonian Institution Press: Washington, DC.
Lamb, Julia. "The Commodore James Gordon Bennett." November 1978: 132. *Smithsonian* Institution Press: Washington, DC.
The *National Aeronautics Association*, Report 1933. Washington, DC.
Orman, Ward T. van. 1978. *The Wizard of the Winds*. Saint Cloud, Minnesota: North Star Press
Schütze, Richard. 1933. Report of Chicago Meet.

Author biography of Stephen Neulander can be found on page 102.

Erich Schröder is a member and officer of the Deutscher Aero Philatelisten Club e.V. and the Kulturgesellschaft Freiballon e.V. in Germany where he resides. He collects Gordon Bennett balloonposts and German airmail of 1919.

12

The Hong Kong Flights

of

Eurasia Airline

by Dr. Peter Moeller

Eurasia Aviation Corporation —A German-Chinese Airline in China

Since its founding days in January 1926, Deutsche Lufthansa Airline was determined to not only establish a dense airmail route structure within Germany and to important European connecting points, but also to expand its service world-wide.

One of these long-distance developments was a route to East Asia. Negotiations for a trans-Eurasian route were made in the late 1920s, but financial and other problems occurred.

Political developments of the time did not permit such an air service by a German airline. To connect the German capital Berlin with Peking, Shanghai, or Tokyo required the help and service of other national airlines along the way.

The Chinese Government and Deutsche Lufthansa thus established a joint venture, an European-Asian company, the Eurasia Aviation Corporation, which could handle the airmail service within China.

The first official airmail flight of this new company, "Eurasia," took place on May 31, 1931.

According to the Chinese Postal Administration Notification No. 37, dated Nanking, May 25, 1931 "The rates of postage on air correspondence (letters and postcards) chargeable on articles to be transmitted from Shanghai or Nanking or any intermediary office along the Shanghai—Manchouli air line, to any European Country will be supplied at any Post Office counter. Airmails to Europe will close twice weekly on Saturdays and Tuesdays at Nanking Head and Sub-Offices."

A Junkers F-13 left Shanghai on May 31 for Peking. There the mail was transferred to a W-33 which left a few hours later for Linsi. The flight continued the next day to Manchouli, a town on the Chinese-Soviet border, where the first flight of Eurasia ended on June 1, 1931. The mail was transferred to the Trans-Siberian Railroad. In Irkutsk, mail was taken off the train and flown by the newly formed Soviet Airline W.O.G.W.F. to Moscow. The Deruluft Airline took over and flew the mail on the last leg, the Moscow—Königsberg—Berlin route. Travel time for mail from Shanghai to Berlin was about eight days.

It is not confirmed if mail was carried on the Eurasia Airline part of the route from Manchouli back to Shanghai, and it is very doubtful that mail from Europe was part of the pay load. The official German postal announcement, *Verfügung Nr. 264,* did not appear until June 16.

During the summer of 1931, however, the airmail route from Berlin to the Far East had to be suspended due to an Eurasia mail plane having been shot down and the occupation of Manchuria by Japanese Forces.

Since Deutsche Lufthansa did not wish to withdraw completely from China, other ways to connect Shanghai with Berlin by air had to be found by Eurasia Airline.

Until the summer of 1937, most attempts seemed to be in vain. But during this time of growth, Eurasia was successful in establishing a well functioning network within China, even though the concept deviated from the basic thoughts of the founding days. Eurasia was just not able to connect to an "international transfer point."

The First Eurasia Connection to Hong Kong

During the 1930s, the world's aviation network began to develop and expand internationally. In the spring of 1936, the British airline Imperial Airways expanded its route to Southeastern Asia and to Hong Kong. This expansion meant that Eurasia finally came much closer to an international connecting point.

Two years earlier, the route between Peking (at the time the city was called Peiping), and Canton was flown regularly. Technical reasons were given when this scheduled flight was stopped.

But now that Imperial Airways had expanded its services, the route to Canton became of interest again.

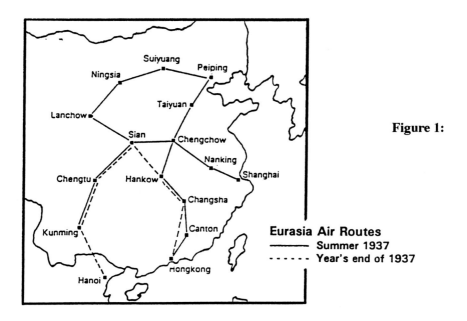

Figure 1:

Eurasia Air Routes
——— **Summer 1937**
- - - - - - **Year's end of 1937**

The British Government gave its permission for Eurasia's airplanes to fly across the Chinese border on June 29, 1937. Fifteen passengers were on this flight by a German air carrier from Peking to Hong Kong, flying the distance of 1,450 miles in just over twelve hours. Finally, connection could be made to Europe and across the Pacific Ocean with Pan American Airways, via Manila to the United States. With the help of Imperial Airways, mail from China to Germany and return could reach its destination in about eight days (Figure 2).

Mail carried on this first flight is known not only from Peking, but also from all intermediate stops as well (Taiyuan, Chengchow, Hankow, Changsha, and Canton).

The return flight from Peking the following day (June 30, 1937) can also be documented with first flight covers.

It is not known how many flights were flown by Eurasia Airline between Peking and Hong Kong. We are reasonably sure that this connection existed only for a very short time. Many first flight covers, official and private, are known from the June 29, 1937 flight, but there is hardly any commercial mail known from later flights (Figure 3).

The Sino-Japanese War Influenced Eurasia Flights

The outbreak of the Sino-Japanese War on July 7, 1937, influenced the future and changed the routes of all Eurasia flights. Only one week after opening its new Hong Kong route, Japan attacked China. All flights from Peking were canceled.

During the next few months, many of the intermediate stops were occupied by Japanese troops. The port of Shanghai was closed, no vital supplies (maintenance parts and fuel) from Germany could be delivered to Eurasia Airline. Other harbors were soon suffering under the Japanese blockade; only Hong Kong, the British Crown Colony, was excluded.

As the main administration office and headquarters of Eurasia were moved at the outbreak of the war from Shanghai to Sian (today Xian), Hong Kong and its connection to the rest of the world were of vital importance.

On August 30, 1937, the route Sian—Hankow—Changsha—Canton— Hong Kong was opened. Vital supplies from Germany could now be delivered via the harbor of Hong Kong. The return flight took place the following day.

No aerophilatelic records are known so far of mail having been carried on the flight to Hong Kong; and only a very small number of covers were carried on the return flight (Figure 4).

Figure 2: First Flight from Peking to Hong Kong, on June 29, 1937.

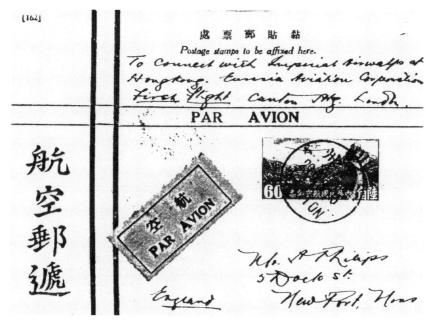

Figure 3: First Eurasia air connection from Canton to London via Hong Kong on June 29, 1937. The Hong Kong transit marking was applied on July 2, 1937, at 8:30 A.M.

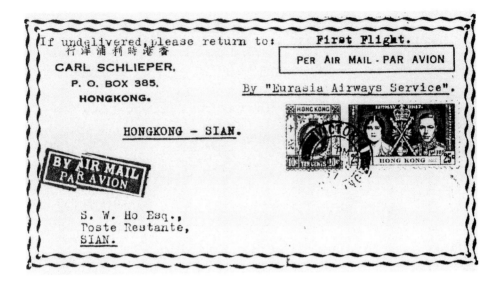

Figure 4: First Flight cover flown from Hong Kong to Sian on August 31, 1937, showing the arrival cancel of September 1, 1937.

Late in September 1937, the German Consulate received threats from the Japanese towards Eurasia. It was decided to move headquarters again, this time to the less vulnerable southern city of Kunming, a town in the Province of Yunan. In an internal report the then President of Eurasia, Kurt Holtz, wrote "In Kunming, Eurasia found a bad airfield and nothing else." It took a year until the new center was fully functional again and a route from Kunming could be opened to Hong Kong. Until that time, all mail had to be flown from Kunming via Chengtu, Sian, Hankow, and Changsha to Hong Kong. All mail from China destined for Europe, had to be flown on this route.

An interesting envelope is shown in Figure 5. The cover was posted in Hankow on July 11, 1938, and is addressed to Stuttgart, Germany. A transit postmark was applied in Hong Kong on July 12. One can see in the upper left hand section an oval double bar marking which gives additional information about the means of transportation. According to articles by Frans van Beveren in which partly flown covers were researched, this marking was used in Marseille, France. This marking means that the cover shown was not flown as originally scheduled with KLM, but with Air France.

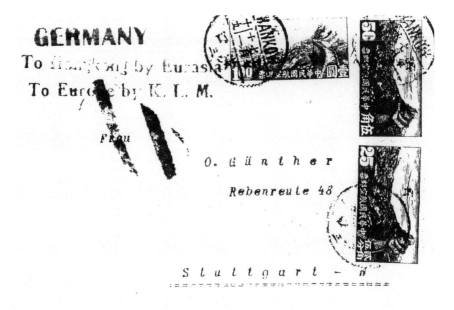

Figure 5: Commercial mail flown from Hankow to Germany via Hong Kong and Marseille, France.

There was no regular French airmail connection on July 12, 1938, but an experimental flight was executed by Air France on July 13 from Hanoi to Hong Kong, returning to Hanoi the next day. It seems that this cover was flown to Hanoi and forwarded on the Air France Indochina route to Marseille.

A new short route from Kunming via Liuchow to Hong Kong was opened on June 13, 1938, in addition to the already existing route from Hankow to Changsha, Canton and Hong Kong.

The British Government however, gave permission only for the route from Hankow to Changsha, Canton and to Hong Kong. Thus the route via Liuchow had to be stopped after only a few flights. To find commercial mail (Figure 6) carried on this route should be extremely challenging to the aerophilatelist.

As Japanese troops advanced toward Canton in August of 1938, the airport in the British crown colony could be reached only during the night. Night flights as such were unheard of in Chinese civil aviation.

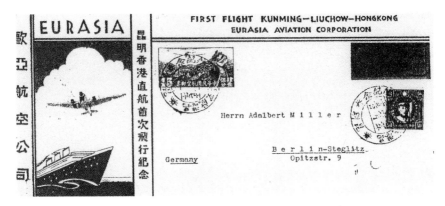

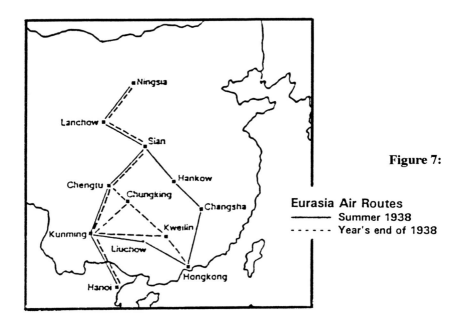

Figure 6: First Flight from Kunming via Liuchow to Hong Kong with Eurasia Airline, and from Hong Kong with Imperial Airways to London, England.

Figure 7:

Eurasia Air Routes
——— Summer 1938
- - - - - - Year's end of 1938

In October 1938, Hankow and Canton were surrendered and Hong Kong was isolated from the Chinese mainland.

Since this development was expected, preparations had already been made to route the flights to Hong Kong via Kweilin (today it is called Guilin). This route, Kunming—Chungking—Kweilin—Hong Kong, was also flown mostly at night.

World War II Destroys Eurasia Aviation Corporation

Even though there was a threat of war in Europe and a growing hostility between Germany and Great Britain, Eurasia continued to fly over hostile Japanese-occupied territory.

The British Government had guaranteed safety to all German personnel, if the expected outbreak of war should find them in Hong Kong. But the German Government in Berlin stopped all flights just prior to the outbreak of World War II.

The Eurasia Airline was able to make an arrangement with the British Government to continue flying into Hong Kong if only Chinese flying personnel were employed. In December 1939, flights did go again to Hong Kong and continued during 1940 and 1941.

After the Japanese attack on Pearl Harbor on December 7, 1941 and the declaration of war by the United States, Great Britain, and China, Japanese troops occupied the city of Hong Kong on December 23, 1941.

All Eurasia's flights to Hong Kong were suspended. The war had closed another chapter in international aerophilatelic development.

On June 1, 1943, Eurasia Airline was liquidated. Technical problems were solved to reach across the Asian Continent, but human and political problems could not be solved.

Bibliography:

van Beveren, Frans J. "Markings on partly flown covers." *The Airpost Journal.* Vol 60 (May 1989) no 8: 268-273, Vol 60 (June 1989) no 9: 324-328.

Holtz, Kurt. "Eurasia Aviation Corporation. *Jahresbericht 1937, Jahresbericht 1939.* Archive of the German Lufthansa Airline. Cologne, Germany.

Moeller, Dr. Peter. 1989. *Eurasia Aviation Corporation, die Entwicklung der Fluggesellschaft und ihre Luftpost, China 1931—1943. Aerophilatelistisches Handbuch und Katalog* (The development of the airline and its airmail service, an aerophilatelic handbook and catalogue). Published by the author: Filderstadt, Germany.

Muller, Frank. 1950. *Catalogue des Aérogrammes du Monde Entier.* Paris, France. Reprinted by FISA in 1970.

Sieh, Pingwen and J. Lewis Blackburn. 1981. *Postage Rates of China, 1867—1980.* Published In Celebration of the 70th Anniversary of the Founding of the Republic of China. Taipei, Taiwan: Directorate General of Posts.

Article translated by Simine Short.

Dr. Peter Moeller is an aerophilatelic researcher of mail flown from and to mainland China. He serves as President of the European Aerophilatelic Club (EAPC) and as editor for its *Bulletin* in Stuttgart, Germany. He has written many articles about Chinese airmail. His column, "Aerophilatelic Literature in Review," received the FISA Literature Medal in 1987. Dr. Moeller is exhibiting nationally and internationally.

13

The New Zealand Survey Flights, Conducted by Pan American Airways

by **Greg Schmidt**

The inauguration of regular airmail service to the South Pacific took place on July 12, 1940. The *American Clipper* (NC18606), a Boeing 314, departed from San Francisco for the trip south. The islands of Hawaii were reached on July 13. The flight continued the following day to Canton Island, and to Noumea, New Caledonia, on the 15th and 16th. The final leg of the flight left for Auckland, New Zealand, on July 18. The return flight departed New Zealand on July 20, arriving back in San Francisco on July 24, 1940.

Work on surveying possible routes across the Pacific ocean began as early as 1931. In July 1931, Colonel and Mrs. Charles Lindbergh made a survey flight for Pan American from New York to China in a Lockheed Sirius, flying via Alaska, Siberia, and Japan. But the Soviet Union would not allow American aircraft to use bases in Siberia, so other solutions had to be found to cross the Pacific Ocean.

The United States Navy was concerned over the expansionism of Japan in the Pacific area. The islands of the South Pacific might become pivotal in the event of an armed conflict; but they could also act as a shield for the Hawaiian Islands and the Panama Canal, and as a stepping stone in the alternate route to Australia, in case the island of Guam was overtaken.

Pan American Airways had conducted several survey flights to Hawaii, Midway, Wake, and Guam during 1935. Regular airmail service (FAM 14) was initiated on November 22, 1935.

The original route to the South Pacific and Australia, as it was proposed by Pan Am, went from Hawaii to Brisbane. Australia, with intermediate stops at Canton Island and Fiji, a British Crown Colony. A less direct route would include Hawaii, American-held Kingman Reef, American Samoa, and New Zealand.

The direct route to the South Pacific was blocked by the British, with Qantas and Imperial Airways acting as partners. The British route to Hong Kong was to continue via Brisbane, Australia, across the Pacific to Vancouver, Canada, across the North American continent, then connect with their Atlantic service.

With the direct route to New Zealand via Canton Island and Fiji being put on hold, the less direct route to New Zealand via Kingman Reef and American Samoa took center stage.

The Hawaiian Islands became the pivotal point for all of Pan American's Pacific operations. And the United States Government refused landing permission to foreign air carriers.

At an Imperial Air Conference (September 1936) in New Zealand, the British reiterated their demand that unlimited landing rights in Hawaii be obtained from the United States Government before any similar rights were accorded to Pan American in Australia and New Zealand.

The route to New Zealand continued to be blocked by the New Zealand Government, which had inserted a clause into the 1936 contract with Pan American Airways, that permitted termination of the contract in the event a British air carrier was refused permission to land at an United States airport.

One year lapsed. There were equipment shortages, but Pan Am was also plagued by various problems in the mid-Pacific. Pan Am requested an extension to its contract with New Zealand.

But the New Zealand Government tried to hold Pan Am to the clause in the contract that no extension would be granted without a promise that Pan Am would use its presumed influence with the United States Government to secure reciprocal landing privileges for Imperial Airways.

The need for an aerial connection to the outside world was the overriding issue in New Zealand's final granting of the extension, while reminding Pan Am that their obligation was "entirely one of honor."

With this extension at hand, hasty preparations were made to survey the route to the South Pacific and to New Zealand.

Survey flights are required to assess the feasibility of each stop on a proposed route by an airline, in this case Pan American Airways. Information is gathered regarding meteorological conditions, water-landing sites at each island proposed, flying time estimates with fuel requirements between each stop, as well as alternate landing sites.

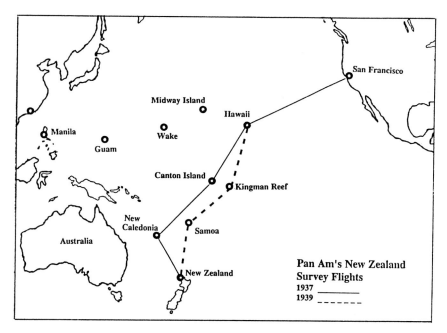

Figure 1: The 1937 and 1939 survey flights by Pan American Airways.

The 1937 New Zealand Survey Flights

Prior to the establishment of the actual air service, Pan Am conducted three survey flights. The first flights were staged between March and April of 1937. The second survey flight took place in December 1937, and January 1938. The third and final survey was conducted in August and September, 1939. The 1937 and 1939 routes are shown in Figure 1.

On March 11, 1937, New Zealand conceded full commercial traffic rights to Pan American, and six days later Pan Am headed to New Zealand on the first survey flight.

The *Pan Am Clipper II* (NC16734), a Sikorsky S42B, was flown from Alameda, California, to Hawaii, March 17-18, 1937. On March 23, the clipper departed from Hawaii for Kingman Reef, arriving later the same day. The flight from American Samoa to New Zealand took place on March 28 and 29, 1937.

The return flight left New Zealand on April 4, reaching American Samoa on the 3rd. The flight had crossed the International Date Line, thus the apparent loss of one day. The flight proceeded to Kingman Reef and reached the Hawaiian Islands on April 9.

The airplane used for this survey flight did not return to Alameda, but was used again in the middle of April for the survey flight to Manila, Philippines, and Hong Kong, after being renamed the *Hong Kong Clipper*.

Pan American Airways departed Hawaii on December 23, 1937, for the second survey flight, reaching Auckland, New Zealand, on December 26. Kingman Reef and American Samoa were intermediate landing points, as in the first survey flights.

To maintain its franchise with the government of New Zealand, Pan Am was under contract to carry mail on the flight back to the United States. Due to mechanical problems, along with inclement weather, the flight did not depart Auckland until January 2, 1938.

Mail carried on the return flight was posted at several post offices between December 24 and 31, 1937.

A complete listing was recently published in *The Bulletin of the Metropolitan Air Post Society*, showing all post offices recorded to date which processed mail, along with times, dates, and other pertinent information.

Figure 2: T/O No.1292a. Auckland—Samoa—Kingman Reef—Hawaii. 353 pieces sent by registered mail to Hawaii.

Figure 3: T/O No. 1292. Auckland — Samoa.

On January 2, 1938, the *Samoan Clipper* (NC16734), a Sikorsky S42B, the same plane as was used on the March 1937 survey flights, departed for Pago Pago, Samoa. The flight crossed the International Date Line, reached Samoa on January 1, proceeded to Kingman Reef, and reached Hawaii on January 3.

At Hawaii, all mail was transferred to the *Philippine Clipper* (NC14715), a Martin 130 flying boat, for the flight to Alameda, back on the North American mainland.

Mail carried on the return flight reached all points along the route, except for Kingman Reef, where there is no dispatch recorded to date.

The following is a listing of the airmail rates for mail dispatched from New Zealand for the survey flight northeast.

Destination	Letter Rate	Postcard Rate	Registration
Samoa	6 P	3 P	4 P
Hawaii	3 Sh	1 Sh 6 P	4 P
Alameda	4 Sh 6 P	2 Sh 3 P	4 P

Figures 2 and 3 (shown on the previous page) show examples of mail as it is recorded in the *American Air Mail Catalogue,* Trans-Oceanic Flight T/O No. 1292a and T/O No. 1292.

The following is a listing of the variety of T/O No. 1292 with the black cachet, recorded to date. The covers were postmarked at Auckland on December 28 or 29, 1937.

The examples described here will be identified as a newly discovered variety of these listings, T/O No. 1292 and T/O No. 1292a. These flown covers have a black cachet measuring $2^1/_2$ by $1^1/_2$ inches (Figure 4).

All but one of the envelopes are the No. 10 large size, some are autographed by Captain Edwin Musick, pilot of the *Samoan Clipper.*

All but one of the covers were addressed to the Pan American Airways Company. The cachet was designed by Pan Am.

Figure 4: T/O No.1292. New Zealand — Samoa leg of flight.

Destination	Franking	Pilot autographed	Total
American Samoa	6 p	5	11
Hawaii	3 Sh	1	3
Alameda	4 Sh 6 p	6	10
Total		12	24

The following are the figures compiled by the New Zealand Post Office for mail dispatched for the 1937 New Zealand Survey Flight:

Destination	Ordinary Mail	Registered Mail	Total
Samoa	5,185	702	5,887
Hawaii	3,172	353	3,525
Alameda	12,814	2,908	15,722
Total:			25,134

All mail dispatched from New Zealand received an official rubber cachet reading " NEW ZEALAND - U.S.A / FIRST AIR MAIL/ DECEMBER, 1937." The cachet was to be applied in red, but some mail received the cachet in purple.

Fifty-two covers have been recorded to date with the purple cachet.

Shown in Figure 5 is one of these covers with the official cachet, applied by the New Zealand Post Office.

Figure 5: Timaru, New Zealand, posted December 27, 1937, for the first flight to the United States, flown onwards to Canada. Official cachet was applied to all mail destined from New Zealand to the United States.

With the success of the New Zealand Survey Flights, Pan American was now ready to inaugurate its regular air service to the South Pacific.

The following is a break-down of mail recorded to date which received the elusive purple cachet:

City of Dispatch	Date & Time posted		Mail Type
Auckland	Dec 28, 1937	8 P.M.	Ordinary
Auckland	Dec 28, 1937	1 P.M.	Registered
Timaru	Dec 27, 1937	7 A.M.	Ordinary
Wellington	Dec 24, 1937	6 P.M.	Ordinary
Wellington	Dec 28, 1937	9 A.M.	Ordinary
Wellington	Dec 28, 1937	11 A.M.	Ordinary
Wellington	Dec 28, 1937	2 P.M.	Ordinary
Wellington	Dec 28, 1937	8 P.M.	Ordinary
Wellington	Dec 29, 1937	2 P.M.	Ordinary

The first flight departed Hawaii for Kingman Reef on January 9, 1938. No official mail was carried on this flight, as the United States Post Office Department had not yet granted Pan American Airways a permit to carry official mail.

The flight left Kingman Reef on January 10 for Samoa.

Mechanical difficulties developed after take-off the following day. The crew radioed back to Samoa that they would be returning but that they had to dump part of their gasoline supply before trying to land. During the unloading process, a spark ignited the gasoline vapors, destroying the *Samoan Clipper* and all hands on board.

With the loss of Captain Edwin Musick and the *Samoan Clipper*, Pan Am suspended all flights to the South Pacific until August 1939.

The 1939 New Zealand Survey Flights

Developing and then maintaining airmail service to the South Pacific began again with the survey flight conducted by Pan American Airways in August 1939.

The *California Clipper* (NC18602), a Boeing 314, left San Francisco on August 22, 1939, arriving in Hawaii the next day.

The 1939 survey flights used Canton Island and Noumea, New Caledonia, rather than Kingman Reef and Samoa, which were used in the earlier survey flights. The main reason for the change of bases was the introduction of the longer range Boeing Flying Boats early in 1939.

The flight southwest departed from the Hawaiian Islands to Canton Island on August 24, 1939. It continued onwards, departing Canton Island on August 27, and arriving at New Caledonia on the 28th.

The final leg of the southbound flight left on August 30 and reached New Zealand later the same day.

Mail carried on the 1939 New Zealand survey flight has been documented in the *American Air Mail Catalogue* as mail dispatched from Canton Island on the return flight to the United States. Four pieces have been recorded to date which were prepared for the southbound flight, with all four covers being posted at Honolulu on August 23, 1939 at 11 A.M. As no airmail contract existed at the time, mail sent to New Caledonia had postage added at Noumea, New Caledonia, to receive a (departure or arrival) postmark.

Mail sent to New Zealand was carried round-trip from Hawaii to New Zealand and back to Hawaii, qualified by the additional postage added at New Zealand for the northbound leg of the survey flight. New Zealand postage was used as no airmail contract existed at the time with the United States.

The currently known four covers were franked with 6 cents United States airmail and were posted at Honolulu, Hawaii.

The New Caledonia covers were franked with a total of 2 franc and 75 centimes postage.

Two pence postage was used on New Zealand mail.

Figures 6 and 7 show mail flown on the southbound leg of the New Zealand survey flight.

The return flight left Auckland on September 2, 1939, and arrived at New Caledonia later the same day. The flight continued on September 4 from Noumea, crossed the International Date Line and arrived at Canton Island on September 3. The final leg of the flight departed Hawaii on September 5, reaching San Francisco the next day.

Figure 6: Hawaii—New Caledonia leg of 1939 New Zealand Survey Flight on August 24 through 28, 1939. Two recorded to date.

Figure 7: Hawaii—New Zealand—Hawaii leg of 1939 New Zealand survey flight on August 24 through September 4, 1939, two recorded to date (John L. Johnson, Jr. collection).

Mail carried on the return flight from Canton Island via Hawaii to San Francisco is catalogued in the *American Air Mail Catalogue* as Trans-Oceanic Flight T/O No. 1329.

Mail from Canton Island was carried either in a pilot's pouch or flown to Hawaii to be postmarked, as no post office existed at Canton Island at the time.

Flown mail was postmarked on September 5 at either 11 or 11:30 A.M. at Honolulu, Hawaii. One flown cover is currently known postmarked on September 8, 1939 at 11:30 A.M..

The following table lists all mail recorded to date which was dispatched from Canton Island with the envelope size, time posted, cachet color (black or violet), franking, and destination.

Table 1: T/O No. 1329. Flown mail dispatched from Canton Island and postmarked in Hawaii;

Envelope (Total)	Time Posted	Cachet Color	Franking	Destination
#6 (2)	11:00 A.M.	black	$ .20	San Francisco
#6 (1)	11:00 A.M.	black	$ .18	Hawaii
#6 (4)	11:30 A.M.	black	$ .20	San Francisco
#6 (1)	11:30 A.M.	violet	$ .20	San Francisco
#6 (1)	11:30 A.M.	black	$ .03	San Francisco
#10 (1)	11:30 A.M.	violet	$ .03	Hawaii
#10 (2)	11:30 A.M.	black	$ .20	San Francisco
#10 (1)	11:30 A.M.	black	$ .03	Hawaii
#10 (1)	11:30 A.M.	black	$ .20	Hawaii
#10 (1)	11:30 A.M.	black	$ .03	San Francisco
#10 (1)	11:30 A.M.	violet	$ .20	San Francisco
#10 (1)	11:30 A.M.	black	$ .20	Guam

Mail is divided into two separate categories:

• Mail postmarked in Hawaii (T/O No. 1329) and

• Mail handstamped with a six-line blue cachet, attesting to the validity of the cover, with the signature by the Airways Superintendent at Canton Island, F. McKenzie.

There is a total of fourteen flown covers with a black cachet and three with a violet cachet currently known.

Table 2: T/O No. 1329. Flown mail dispatched from Canton Island and handstamped at Canton Island:

Envelope (Total)	Cachet Color	Destination
#6 (4)	black	San Francisco
#10 (1)	black	San Francisco
#10 (2)	violet	San Francisco

Figure 8: T/O No. 1329. Canton Island—Hawaii—San Francisco. Carried in pilot's pouch. Blue six-line handstamp with violet flight cachet applied at Canton Island.

Five flown covers are currently known with a black cachet and two covers with a violet cachet.

The grand total of all recorded covers, flown from Canton Island to different destinations is twenty-four, with seventeen covers posted in Hawaii and seven showing the private Canton Island handstamp.

Figures 8 and 9 show both varieties of T/O No. 1329.

With the invaluable groundwork laid by the 1937 and 1939 New Zealand Survey Flights, Pan American Airways was able to commence regular airmail service to the South Pacific on July 12, 1940.

The airmail rates for the inaugural service are listed below.

Airmail Rates for the New Zealand Inaugural Service:

Departure Point	Destination	Airmail rate
San Francisco	Canton Island	$ .30
	New Caledonia	$ .40
	New Zealand	$ .50
Hawaii	Canton Island	$ .10
	New Caledonia	$ .20
	New Zealand	$ .30
Canton Island	San Francisco	$ .30
	Hawaii	$ .10
	New Caledonia	$ .10
	New Zealand	$ .20
New Caledonia *	San Francisco	19.50 Fr
	Hawaii	11 Fr
	Canton Island	7 Fr
	New Zealand	7 Fr
New Zealand	San Francisco	4 Sh
	Hawaii	2 Sh 6 p
	Canton Island	2 Sh
	New Caledonia	1 Sh 6 p

* Note: New Caledonian postage was a combination of letter rate and airmail rate.

Figure 9: T/O No. 1329. Canton Island—Hawaii—San Francisco, showing the black flight cachet.

Bibliography:

Bender, Marilyn and Selig Altschul. 1982. The chosen instrument: Juan Trippe, Pan Am, the rise and fall of an American Entrepreneur. New York, New York: Simon and Schuster.

Crampon, L.J. "Aerophilatelic Flights, Hawaii & Central Pacific, 1913-1946." (November 1980). Honolulu, Hawaii: Hawaiian Philatelic Society.

Daley, Robert. 1980. *An American Saga, Juan Trippe and his Pan Am Empire*. New York, New York: Random House.

Davies, R. E. G. 1972. *Airlines of the United States, since 1914*. Washington, DC: Smithsonian Institution Press.

Lüning, Orjan et al. 1981."Trans-Oceanic Record Flights." *American Air Mail Catalogue*. Vol 4 ed 5: 15350-1608. Cinnaminson, New Jersey: American Air Mail Society.

Schmidt, Greg. "Pan American Airways: the route to New Zealand." *1990 COMPEX Directory*, Vol 33: 103-115. Chicago, Illinois.

----- "The 1937 New Zealand survey flight dispatch points." *The Bulletin of the Metropolitan Air Post Society*. Vol 6 (October/December 1991) no 4: 9-10.

----- "New Caledonia airmail rates in 1940-1941." *The Airpost Journal*. Vol 61 (January 1990) no 1: 18-19.

----- "Canton Island and Wake Island survey flights." *The Airpost Journal.* Vol 60 (November/December 1989) no 14: 540.

----- "21 Canton Island survey flight covers reported." *The Airpost Journal.* Vol 60 (March 1989) no 7: 216-218.

Walker, Douglas A. 1986. "The Overseas Flights, 1928-1940." Vol 2, *The Airmails of New Zealand.* Christchurch, New Zealand: The Airmail Society of New Zealand:

United States Postal Service, Archives.

Pan American Airways, Archives.

Greg Schmidt is a member of the Board of the American Air Mail Society and the AAMS Publications Sales Manager. He collects and studies the development of airmail and passenger service to the Pacific area by Pan American Airways, 1935-1941, including the naval forerunner period (1925-1935). Memberships include the American Air Mail Society, Aerophilatelic Federation of the Americas, American Philatelic Society and American Association of Philatelic Exhibitors.

14

Winged Cargo,

One of Many Non-Skeds

by Simine Short

In May 1946, Winged Cargo received a Civil Aeronautics Board "Letter of Registration" for commercial, non-scheduled glider towing operations between Philadelphia and Puerto Rico. This permitted the uncertificated air carrier (according to the CAB those air carriers not operating under federal "certificates" were termed "uncertificated") to fly passengers and cargo from any point in the United States and its possessions, and cargo only to foreign countries on "irregular" or "unscheduled" trips.

The story of Winged Cargo and the hundreds of other Non-scheduled (or Non-Sked), Irregular, Charter, or Supplemental Carriers just after World War II, is full of controversy and many facts are still quite obscure. This section of aviation and airline history still needs additional research. The aerophilatelic coverage is hampered by the fact that "official" mail was not authorized to be carried by these non-scheduled and/or non-certificated air carriers.

On October 18, 1938, non-scheduled air carriers were exempted from having to obtain a "Certificate of Public Convenience and Necessity." Thus, this Civil Aeronautics Act established not only grounds for certificating the major air carriers, but it also provided for exemptions allowing a development of experimental and uncertificated air transport. Among the experiments authorized by the Act, was a framework for scheduled "feeder airlines." These were to feed passengers, mail, and cargo to and from small communities to the main trunk lines.

All American Aviation, Inc., was the first certificated feeder airline and the only one before World War II. Its experimental pick-up operation was an excellent example of how the air service could expand to smaller communities which heretofore had no scheduled air service. The inaugural flight of experimental route No.1002 from Latrobe, Pennsylvania, to Pittsburgh, Pennsylvania, carried sixty pounds of mail, including the letter shown in Figure 1 which then continued to its destination by airmail on board a major carrier. This experimental service proved highly successful. In 1940, All American received the contract for regular service under CAM 49.

A dramatic change in the operations of the non-sked carriers occurred during and after World War II. Larger cargo-carrying planes emerged from the war effort of flying personnel and materiel over mountain peaks and open seas. In the immediate post-war period, the government released thousands of G.I.s who were experienced in using the larger aircraft. Many small cargo airlines (also known as "G.I. Airlines") were founded. These airlines purchased, usually for a nominal sum, surplus aircraft from the War Assets Board. For many former pilots it was a dream come true to run their own airline and continue flying.

On May 17, 1946, the Civil Aeronautics Board modified the 1938 exemption regulations. An expanded level of air transport service was to be permitted. Non-scheduled carriers, with only a CAB Letter of Registration, were now authorized to engage in interstate and overseas transport of persons and property between any two points, but only on an infrequent and irregular basis. *Air Transport* lists 194 "Contract Carriers in the United States" in its July 1946 issue. According to R.E.G. Davies, during this period there were over 2,000 uncertificated air carriers of all varieties flying in the United States.

In the spring of 1947, the Civil Aeronautics Board gave uncertificated air carriers a fully defined official status, establishing the "irregular air carrier" (revision of the *CAB's Economic Regulations*: section 292.1: engage in common carriage by air, as long as it is on an irregular basis, of persons and property domestically and property alone internationally) and the "non-certificated cargo carrier" (section 292.5: who may act as common carriers of property only, on a regular or irregular basis, in interstate commerce, but not internationally).

In spite of many shortcomings, the young non-scheduled airline industry began to provide evidence that it could make a significant contribution to airline progress. The same month World War II came to an end, the newly formed Flying Tiger air carrier flew two cargoes of fresh vegetables from California to Detroit, Michigan, and to Atlanta, Georgia.

Figure 1: Experimental Route No.1002, a non-stop pick-up and delivery service. Cover was picked up in Latrobe, Pennsylvania, on May 12, 1939, and flown to Pittsburgh, Pennsylvania, by All American Aviation. Cachet shows the pick-up device.

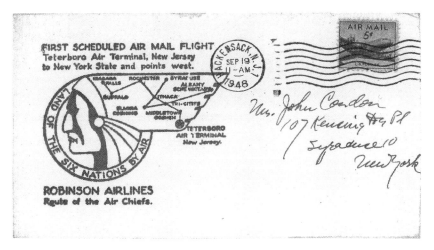

Figure 2: September 19, 1948, Hackensack, New Jersey. Robinson Airlines, "Route of the Air Chiefs, confirms with this special First Flight cover the inauguration of Certificated Airline Transportation."

An interesting example of a non-scheduled charter operation which became a certificated "feeder" airline was C.S. Robinson, flying chartered three- and four-passenger airplanes from Ithaca, New York, to Teterboro, New Jersey. Robinson Airlines was incorporated in 1946, became certificated as a feeder airline in 1948, became Mohawk Airlines in 1952, and is now part of USAir. Official mail was carried by Robinson Airlines on the inaugural flight (on a three-year temporary certificate) as a feeder airline and the first flight of CAM 94 between New York and Buffalo, New York, on September 19, 1948. Some covers from this flight show the unofficial cachet of Robinson Airlines (Figure 2), others the official United States Post Office cachet.

Some of the non-sked air carriers that did not become trunk airlines or feeder carriers still became illustrious names in the airline industry, but most were unable to survive as operating regulations changed.

The War Assets Board at first had only few airplanes for sale, but many cargo gliders. Cargo gliders were cheaper to operate than the powered airplane, and they could carry a big load when attached to an airplane.

Several glider cargo non-skeds started operation in 1945 and 1946. Little is known of them. One small non-sked, a division of DuPont's All American Aviation, specialized in carrying live lobsters. The lobsters were caught off the coast of Massachusetts and flown to Bendix Airport, Teterboro, New Jersey, in a modified Schweizer TG-3A glider. The lobsters were to be sold in New York City. It is not known how long this cargo operation went on.

Another carrier, National Air Cargo Corp., also existed only a few months. Its cargo consisted of Christmas merchandise from several large department stores which was flown in surplus Waco CG-4A troop gliders from St. Louis, Missouri, to the Los Angeles Municipal Airport. The cargo, by the way, was insured by Lloyds of London for US$25,000. It is thought to be the first insurance placed upon glider-borne cargo.

Laister-Kaufmann, also from St. Louis, started its cargo operation with a Douglas B-23 and two CG-4As. The gliders could be loaded with 1,500 pounds of cargo each.

A possibly better documented non-sked using gliders was Winged Cargo of Philadelphia, Pennsylvania. It was formed in March 1946 by a former Colonel of the United States Army Air Force, Fred P. Dollenberg, who had been stationed at Buna, New Guinea, just before Christmas of 1942.

In a newspaper article in the Philadelphia *Evening Bulletin,* Dollenberg reports: "Our troops embattled near Buna were hard pressed for supplies. Delivery of food and ammunition by barge and parachute was not effective. In this crisis, someone suggested to use gliders. A single cargo glider was dispatched to Port Moresby to pioneer the new method for delivering supplies. Loaded with equipment, it was towed northward by a C-47 Army Transport and cut loose near Buna where it made a smooth landing."

Back home, the question arose again: "If gliders can carry freight to soldiers, why could they not be used to deliver commercial freight?"

Dollenberg and his former copilot, now Winged Cargo Vice President Raymond W. Baldwin, were farsighted people who believed in the future of glider cargo operations. Winged Cargo's Secretary/Treasurer, Carl W. Hardic, had flown cargo glider missions in the early days of the European invasion. Now, these three men began to work out details of a glider freight service.

By the spring of 1946 they had purchased from military surplus one C-47 transport plane and three CG-4A cargo gliders. In the beginning of April 1946, Winged Cargo announced that no regular schedule of flights was contemplated by the organization. The frequency and route of trips from Northwest Airport in Philadelphia, Pennsylvania, would be determined by the cargoes. But Winged Cargo was prepared to furnish shuttle service to any point.

In an experiment to test the feasibility of a towed glider cargo operation, Winged Cargo flew 276,000 tomato plants from Tiffin, Georgia, to Reading, Pennsylvania, under a three-month contract with the Campbell Soup company. Having been successful with the initial test, Dollenberg and his crew announced that they would open a glider tow cargo service along the East Coast to the South and to the West Indies.

An aerophilatelist mailed a few covers to Dollenberg and asked to have them carried on Winged Cargo's first flight.

On April 24, 1946, everything was ready. The C-47 transport plane and the cargo glider were loaded with different goods from the Philadelphia area, including Philco radios, for the 2,000+ mile haul to Havana, Cuba, and to San Juan, Puerto Rico. Both airplanes landed safely at the airfield of the Ranch Boyeros in Cuba, delivering there some of the radios for the Philco division in Havana.

The flight continued the next day to San Juan, where, according to local reports, thousands must have gone to the airport at Grand Isle to witness the arrival of this first commercial glider freight operation.

On the return flight, the precious cargo consisted mostly of cases filled with Don Q rum from Puerto Rico!

Arriving back in the office, Winged Cargo President Dollenberg noticed the envelopes which he was to have carried on his first flight. He made sure that they were flown on the second flight, which left Newark, New Jersey, on May 4, 1946. This time, the sky-train landed in Charleston, South Carolina, and in Nassau, Bahamas, prior to arriving at Losey Field near Ponce, San Juan.

The letter, shown in Figure 3, was posted in San Juan, Puerto Rico, on May 7, 1946 . Dollenberg included a short note to Mr. S. Bayer :

> *Dear Mr. Bayer:*
> *I am exceedingly sorry that your request was not accomplished, but in the great rush of detail involved in our first flight, your envelopes were not taken along. I'm sending along a few of your envelopes, on this our second glider flight to Puerto Rico.*
> *Thanking you for your kindness, I am,*
> *Fred P. Dollenberg*
> *President Winged Cargo, Inc.*

Again, the Philco Company shipped radios; several large advertisements appeared in local Puerto Rico newspapers (competitor R.C.A. advertised their shipments of radios in the brand new DC-3 airplanes, flown by Pan American Airways). The cargo on the return flight was again about two-hundred cases of Don Q rum.

It is not at all clear how many pieces of souvenir mail were carried on this second flight. Possibly fewer than ten? Were the remaining envelopes ever flown by glider? As of today, only two such covers are known to the author.

Aviation News reported in February 1947 that Winged Cargo and its passenger division had flown 6,400,000 plane miles up to December 11, 1946, serving the West Indies and Central America and that it had bases in Nassau, Bahamas, and Charleston, South Carolina. However, it is not mentioned if they were still using gliders. Most likely they were not.

On December 8, 1947, Winged Cargo faced Federal Court action as the Civil Aeronautics Board sought to restrain it from carrying passengers overseas in alleged violation of the Civil Aeronautics Act. At that time, Winged Cargo flew passengers twice a week to Nassau and to San Juan, with DC-3s.

Winged Cargo was enjoined from operation on December 16, 1947.

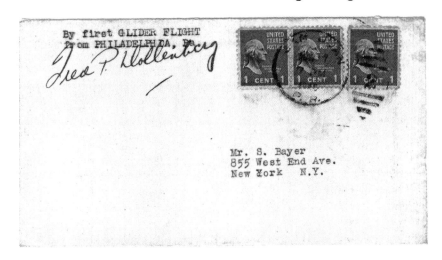

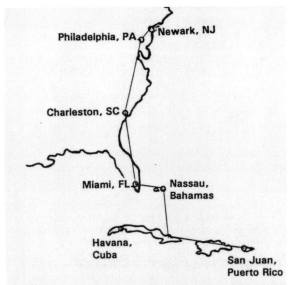

Figure 3: Second flight of Winged Cargo, Inc. from Philadelphia, Pennsylvania, via Newark, New Jersey, to San Juan, Puerto Rico, on May 7, 1946.

Map shows flight route.

The most ambitious commercial glider freight operation had come to an end. Although technologically successful, the towed cargo glider was unable to compete with the efficiency of more readily available modern cargo airplanes. As far as currently known, commercial glider mail has not been attempted since.

The Federal regulation of airlines which was so complex during the late 1940s was almost totally reversed by the United States Airline Deregulation Act of 1978.

Bibliography:

Davies, R.E.G. 1984. *Airlines of the United States since 1914*. Washington, DC: Smithsonian Institution Press.

Diario de la Marina. Havana, Cuba. Miscellaneous issues, April, May, 1946.

Haring, Robert et al. 1977. "United States Official First Flights under Contract or as Designated by the Civil Aeronautics Board." *American Air Mail Catalogue*, Vol 2 ed 5: 899-904. Cinnaminson, New Jersey: American Air Mail Society.

"Independent Operators Swarm To Set Up New Uncertificated Lines." *Aviation News*. Vol 8 (March 4, 1946) no 3: 17-18. New York, New York.

Lewis, W. David and William F. Trimble. 1988. *The Airway to Everywhere, A History of All American Aviation*. Pittsburgh, Pennsylvania: University of Pittsburgh Press.

Mickel, Merlin. "CAB Legalizes Veteran Airlines as 'Irregular and Cargo Carriers'." *Aviation News*. May 19, 1947: 27

Mitchener, Joseph J. Jr. "Feederlines . . and Non-Scheduled Air Carriers, where do they stand in commercial aviation?" *Air Transportation*. Vol 7 (May 1946) no 4: 16-22. New York, New York.

El Mundo. San Juan, Puerto Rico. Miscellaneous issues, April and May, 1946.

"National Air Cargo Glider in First Commercial Flight." *Air Transportation*. Vol 7 (December 1946) no 6: 32. New York, New York.

The New York Times. Miscellaneous issues, 1946 and 1947.

Peach, Robert E. 1964. *Four Seaters to Fan Jets, The Story of Mohawk Airlines, Inc*. An Address to the Newcomen Society in North America on September 24, 1964. New York, New York.

Short, Simine. 1987. *Glider Mail, an Aerophilatelic Handbook*. Cinnaminson, New Jersey: American Air Mail Society.

"Cargo glider versus Cargo Plane and Helicopter." *Soaring* Vol 10 (March/ April 1946) no 3: 4-5.

"United States Non-scheduled Contract Air Carriers and Interstate Airlines." *Air Transportation*. Vol 7 (October 1946) no 5. New York, New York.

Simine Short is an aerophilatelic researcher and collector of glider flown mail. She was a two-term Secretary of the AAMS, has served on several AAMS committees, and has been the AAMS delegate to FISA since 1985. She is also appointed the APS United States Delegate to the FIP Aerophilatelic Commission. Since 1988, she has been Vice President of the Jack Knight Air Mail Society. On a local level, Simine is a Board member of the Chicago Air Mail Society and Exhibits Chair for the CHICAGOPEX exhibitions, was President of the Elmira, New York, Stamp Society. She has written more than 100 articles in English, as well as in German, and has been an invited speaker at international stamp exhibitions. Her first book, *Glider Mail,* was published in 1987 by the AAMS. Her exhibit "Glider Mail, the Pioneering Years," has garnered Gold Medals and Research Awards nationally and internationally, including the Kronfeld Achievement Needle in 1988, presented periodically since 1933 by the Austrian Airmail Collectors Club.

15

Concorde SST:

Flying with the Sun –

Now Flying into the Sunset

by Dr. Reuben A. Ramkissoon

The era of supersonic transport (SST) development was a controversial but eager period in commercial aviation. The first commercial flights by Air France between Paris and Rio de Janeiro via Dakar, and by British Airways between London and Bahrain, initiated regular service on January 21, 1976. Entry into North America followed on May 24, 1976, when Air France and British Airways opened services to Washington, DC, with both aircrafts arriving together on the inaugural service.

Commemorative covers were postmarked at Heathrow Airport, London, the Airport Mail Facility (AMF) at Kennedy International Airport, the General Post Office (GPO), New York, and the United Nations in New York.

A crescendo of vocal American opponents delayed commercial flights to New York until November 22, 1977. Objections were based particularly on the Concorde's noise levels, which were considered dangerous to the populations of airport environs and gateway cities.

The Concorde was built by British Aerospace, the former British Aircraft Corporation. On November 29, 1962, the British and the French Governments signed an agreement for the joint design, construction, and development of a 100-seat aircraft using established materials and techniques. Work on the prototypes began in April 1965; final assembly of the first aircraft began in April 1966; the first Concorde (001) made its initial flight on March 2, 1969.

A long period of development and testing of the prototypes, the French prototype with serial number 001, and the British prototype with serial number 002, followed. The French prototype, 001, flew "with the sun" on June 30, 1973, extending a solar eclipse observation expedition to eighty minutes from Las Palmas on the Canary Islands to Fort Lamy in Chad.

There was early enthusiasm for the project, with an expected sale of 200 aircraft by Anglo-French marketing groups. The United States Federal Aviation Administration (FAA) predicted many more of these SSTs operating from gateways around the world.

Pan American World Airways placed options for six Concordes for its trans-Atlantic route in 1963. But a decade later, the carrier canceled its order citing higher operational costs (160,000 pounds of fuel per Atlantic flight) and less range and payload as compared to the wide-body jet aircraft that were entering the aviation arena.

Pan Am's cancellation initiated an avalanche of rejections by other air carriers. In the end, Air France and British Airways remained the only (self-serving) customers.

A large British government loan for the production of the aircraft in 1968, and the aircraft's cold reception into the world of commercial aviation (a total of sixteen aircraft were ordered), signaled that continuing government support would be necessary to ensure production and delivery.

Covers were carried as "official mail" on only a few Concorde flights.

France authorized only one dispatch and three return mail acceptances. England, France, and the United States did not authorize mail service.

Although Great Britain did not permit Concorde airmail, British Royal Mail Datapost parcel services, whose fees are not postage, circumvented this prohibition. Covers to be forwarded by mail on arrival, required additional postage. 1,368 covers with private printed cachets were flown from London to New York in packets under contracts with Datapost. This service offers parcel delivery by the Concorde from London to New York. Covers and parcel post wrappers exist as company mail.

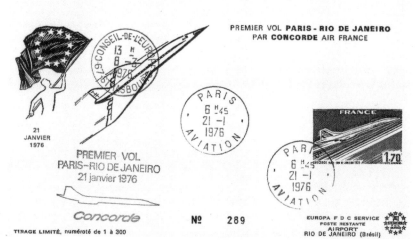

Figures 1: First Commercial Flight by a Concorde from Paris, France, to Rio de Janeiro, Brazil. Top is a French First Flight cover with the 1.70Fr commemorative stamp, while the bottom cover was carried on the return flight, using the special Brazilian stamp, also showing the Concorde.

Great Britain: Royal Mail Datapost Service flown on the Concorde:

Nov 22, 1977	First Passenger Flight: London—New York
Jul 27, 1981	Royal Wedding souvenir flight

France allowed Concorde airmail on only four flights, one round-trip and three return trips. Regular airmail rates applied. Several special stamps, honoring the aircraft Concorde, were issued by France and Brazil.

France: Concorde Airmail Service:

Sep 13, 1971	First Flight: Buenos Aires to Toulouse
Aug 18, 1973	First Flight: Libreville to Toulouse
Jan 21-22, 1976	First Flight: Paris to Rio de Janeiro and return via Dakar, with special French 1.70 Fr and / or Brazil 5.20 Cr stamps
Apr 10, 1976	First Flight: Caracas to Paris

The United States authorized Concorde airmail on only one occasion; however covers to foreign destinations were forwarded by regular contractors.

United States: Concorde Airmail Service

Jan 12-13, 1979	First Flight: Washington to Dallas and return

The majority of Concorde flown covers are commemorative in nature and have been carried as "baggage." The variety and volume of French and British covers carried on such a hand-back basis is amazing In addition to these produced by and for the manufacturers and airlines, a wide selection was carried by philatelic dealers, crew members, and passengers.

In the past few years, promotional "Around the World" flights or flights to various "chartered" locations have received commemorative postmarks. These souvenir flights have helped offset operational losses on the regular service routes of the Concorde .

Philatelic and COMAIL (also known as company mail) are outside the purview of this article. Postage rates charged were those prevailing for airmail service, domestically or to international points. In the few flights where an authorized postal dispatch occurred, the prevailing postage rates had to be applied. COMAIL from Great Britain required no individual letter franking, but postage was charged from the point of entry into the mail.

Review of commemorative and non-authorized "baggage" flown mail indicates the prevailing rates of postage:

Listing of postage rates, used on Concorde flights

Year	Domestic rate	International airmail rate	Aerogramme
France			
1969	.45 Fr	1.00 Fr	
1971	.50 Fr		
1973		1.70 Fr	
1974	.60 Fr		
1975	.80 Fr		
1977	1.90 Fr	1.60 Fr	
1978	1.00 Fr		1.90 Fr
1979			2.10 Fr
1981	1.60 Fr	2.00 Fr	2.35 Fr
1982			2.70 Fr
1983	1.80 Fr	2.30 Fr	3.10 Fr
1984	2.00 Fr		3.30/3.50 Fr
1986	2.20 Fr		3.70/4.20 Fr
Great Britain			
1969	9 d		
1973	3 p		
1974	5 p		
1976	11 p		20 p
1980	13 p		
1981	14 p		
1982	19 p		
1984	22 p		34 p
United States			
1976	13 ¢	22 ¢	
1974	14 ¢	31 ¢	
1979	15 ¢		
1982	20 ¢		
1985	22 ¢		
1989	25 ¢		

The Soviet Union was the only other country to enter the supersonic transport arena. The Tupolev Tu-144 became the first commercial transport to exceed Mach 2, about two months prior to the French 001 prototype's Mach 2 flight. Commercial flights within the Soviet Union occurred one month before the British and French began services.

The Tu-144 made its first commercial flight on December 26, 1975, carrying only freight and mail (Figure 2), inaugurating weekly service between Moscow and Alma Ata.

On November 1, 1977, the first scheduled passenger flights were flown from Moscow to Alma Ata. On August 9, 1984, the Soviet Government announced that the aircraft had been taken out of service.

Figure 2: Souvenir mail prepared for and flown on the First Flight from Moscow to Alma Ata on December 25, 1975 and return to Moscow the following day.

Commemorative airmail stationery envelopes have been issued by the Soviet Postal Service in the series honoring its aircraft (see Figure 3). On November 10, 1988, Andrei N. Tupolev was honored on the centenary of his birth as a famous aeronautical engineer and designer. He designed more than 150 airplanes, from a wooden monoplane to the Tu-144 supersonic 144-seat transport plane.

Figure 3: Airmail postal stationery, issued in honor of Andrei N. Tupolev, designer of the Soviet supersonic air carrier Tu-144.

British Aerospace predicts that the present fleet of Concordes will approach the end of their operational life span by the year 2005, when the aircraft first put into service will reach its 8,000-cycle mark. Unlike subsonic aircraft, which may be able to fly almost indefinitely with proper maintenance, the supersonic Concorde aircraft which operates at or above the speed of sound is subject to greater compression and decompression stresses. For example, due to temperature differences, the aircraft structure may expand and / or contract some nine inches during a flight. As a result of its lack of cost-effectiveness and environmental concerns, no additional supersonic aircraft have been built.

The aerophilatelist who is interested in the era of dramatic supersonic aircraft flights is advised now to locate Concorde mail. Prices are considered high in comparison to other covers of the relatively current period. The Concordes which have flown with the sun, and even ahead of it, are destined to fly into the sunset with the dawn of the next century.

Bibliography:

Barber, Dan. "The Braniff Concorde: An Update." *The Airpost Journal.* Vol 51 (June 1980) no 9: 306-308, 315.

Birger, Larry. "Early Concorde Flight First to Serve Covers." *Linn's Stamp News*. June 26, 1976.

Blumenthal, Frank B. "Mystery USPS Cancel for Concorde." *The Airpost Journal*. Vol 55 (September 1984) no 12: 496.

Cronk, John N. "Controversial Concorde Flies into Philately." *Linn's Stamp News*. March 26, 1979; September 17, 1979; October 29, 1979; April 7, 1980.

Jane's Encyclopedia of Aviation. 1989. Michael J.H. Taylor (ed). New York, New York: Portland House:.

O'Keefe, Donna. "Aerogrammes salute supersonic transport." *Linn's Stamp News*. June, 1981.

Sanford, Kendall C. "London Aerophilatelic Souvenirs." *The Airpost Journal*. Vol 51 (September 1980) no 12: 402-404.

Savadge, David. "AMF-JFK Cancels for 1977 Concorde." *The Airpost Journal*. Vol 54 (November 1982) no 2: 64-65.

Starkweather, Albert W. et al. 1985. "Supersonic Transport, Concorde and Tu-144. First and Special Flights." American Air Mail Catalogue, Vol 5 ed 5: 2567-2580. Cinnaminson, New Jersey: American Air Mail Society.

Starkweather, Albert W. "Concorde—SST Cover Collecting: Some Notes and Listings." *The Airpost Journal*. Part 1: Vol 51 (March 1980) no 6: 184-190. Part 2: Vol 51 (May 1980) no 8: 267-274. Part 3: Vol 51 (September 1980) no 12: 392-396. Part 4: Vol 52 (June 1981) no 9: 302-306. Part 5: Vol 53 (April 1982) no 7: 240-245. Part 6: Vol 54 (October 1982) no 1: 18-22. Part 7: Vol 55 (November 1983) no 2: 69-74. Part 8: Vol 57 (June 1985) no 9: 316-321. Part 9: Vol 58 (December 1985) no 3: 118-121. Part 10: Vol 59 (June 1986) no 8: 326-332.

-----. "Another French Concorde Aerogramme." *The Airpost Journal*. Vol 55 (June 1984) no 9: 379, 381.

-----. "Exploring Harry Gordon's Cachets." *The Airpost Journal*. Vol 55 (May 1984) no 8: 318-319, 342.

-----. "FDCs Enhance Concorde Collection, Expand Aircraft Development Story." *Linn's Stamp News*. November 15, 1982.

-----. "SST Catches on in Aerophilately." *Linn's Stamp News*. Sept 28, 1981.

Stone, Michael. "An Evaluation of Concorde 001 Covers." *The Airpost Journal*. Vol 55 (May 1984) no 8: 338-342.

The author acknowledges the editorial assistance of Albert W. Starkweather, chair of the "Supersonic Transport" section in the *American Air Mail Catalogue*.

Dr. Reuben A. Ramkissoon is President of the Space Topics Study Group, past President of Chicago Air Mail Society and British Caribbean Philatelic Study Group. His specialty fields in aero and astrophilately include jets, development of cosmic mail service, also British Caribbean airmail. Memberships include the AAMS, United Nations Philatelist, Collectors Club of Chicago, Chicago Philatelic Society, and Royal Philatelic Society.

16

The World's

First

Cosmographs

by Les Winick

The Soviet Union has had a manned station in space for many years. At first, it was the Salyut, but this has been replaced with a modern version, named the MIR. The Salyut received cosmonauts from the Soviet Union who stayed on board the space station for as long as eight months. The new station MIR, launched in February 1986, continued and expanded the space station concept as home to crews and foreign space travelers.

Since the cosmonauts were in space for a prolonged period of time, it was arranged for mail to be delivered to them aboard the space station. This consisted of official documents from the space agency and personal mail from the families of the crew.

The mail was usually sent with the next launch vehicle, whether a Progress unmanned spaceship or a manned Soyuz vehicle. The official documents were enclosed in the Soviet version of the inter-office manila envelope used in most commercial firms in the United States. Letters from members of the cosmonauts' relatives were included in the same envelopes.

In either case, no postage stamps were used, nor were there any official postal markings since the letters and agency communications did not go through the normal channels of the mail system.

Collectors should be very cautious if offered examples of this mail and should ask for some sort of certificate from the official government space agency Glavkosmos or Mezhdunarodnaya Kniga attesting to the fact that the item was indeed carried into space.

There are many Soviet covers that are claimed to have been carried to the space stations via the cosmonauts. These frequently have an elaborate printed cachet and an "on-board" cancel, and are usually autographed by the cosmonauts. As of this date, there is no absolute verification that these covers have actually been postmarked on-board the space station. The Russian export agency, Mezhdunarodnaya Kniga, says that they were postmarked in space, but offers no certificates with the covers. One suggestion is that the canceling device may have been the item carried in space. It then was used to cancel the covers back on earth.

The wholesale price of these commemorative covers to large stamp dealers is in the $5 range, so it is doubtful if the heavy covers were permitted on board a space vehicle where every ounce of weight is critical.

In any case, these space covers are very desirable items. They document the launch of the space vehicle and are usually postmarked at the space lift-off site.

In November 1988, the U.S.S.R. Ministry of Communications opened an official post office on board the orbital complex MIR for the receipt and sending of the cosmonauts' official and private mail. A special on-board calendar postmark was manufactured and delivered to the space station.

As verification of mail carried in space, a registered receipt was issued from the Baikonour Cosmodrome. To celebrate the opening of the world's first space post office, 500 sets of post cards were prepared.

The following is the official Soviet story of this historic event.

To MIR via Progress 41

1. A 15-kopek postage stamp, commemorating the 30th anniversary of the launching of the first Soviet rocket to the moon (Scott No. 5744) was affixed to 500 post cards addressed to the crew of the MIR orbital space station.

2. A 1 ruble postage stamp with a "space mail" overprint (Scott No. 5720) was issued for the special occasion of establishing a postal service between the Earth and the space station.

3. A First Day Cancel commemorating Lunik I, dated January 2, 1989, was applied at the Moscow General Post Office.

4. A Baikonour Cosmodrome postal cancel was applied dated March 16, 1989, commemorating the launching of the unmanned Progress 41 cargo space craft with the sets of cards on board.

5. An official space post office cancel was applied at the space station MIR, dated March 18, 1989.

6. The three Soviet cosmonauts S.K. Krikalev, A.A. Volkov, and V. V. Polyakov signed each of the 500 cards and the Soyuz cards on the reverse side on board the MIR orbital complex.

Figure 1: To MIR via Progress 41

To Earth via Soyuz TM-7

7. The return cards also had a 1-ruble postage stamp affixed with a "space mail" overprint. They were addressed to the Chairman of the USSR Glavkosmos space agency. Upon departure, the official space post office applied a cancel dated April 27, 1989.

8. A normal Dzheskazgan post office postmark was applied on April 27, 1989, when the manned Soyuz TM-7 landed with the cards aboard. A Progress 41 cachet was applied to the cards carried on that space vehicle, and a Soyuz TM-7 cachet was placed on the return cards.

9. The Chairman of Glaskosmos, A.I. Dunaev, signed each of the 500 Progress cards on the reverse side.

10. Each set of cards was serial-numbered from 1 to 500 with a matching registered receipt.

11. The cards were placed in an attractive colorful folder along with the certificates of authenticity.

12. The purchasers of the cards also received a video tape showing the process of canceling and then signing of the cards by the cosmonauts while in space.

Figure 2: To Earth via Soyuz TM-7

The world's first post office in outer space is in operation and a cosmonaut will be named "Postmaster" for each flight.

Postscript

There has been additional news about Soviet flown space mail that should be brought to the attention of all collectors. The German astrophilatelic publication *Weltraum—Philatelie* reported that covers flown on the November 26 through December 21, 1988, French-Soviet flight exist with false postal markings.

The cancellation device was supposed to have been on board the MIR space station during the flight, yet covers exist canceled with the seemingly genuine postmark on dates when the canceling device should have been in space.

Three theories currently exist as to how these covers could have been prepared:

1. The MIR postmark used on these covers is an outright fake;

2. There are two MIR canceling devices, one used on Earth and the other is still in space.

3. The MIR cancel is genuine, but was used by Mezhdunarodnaya Kniga personnel prior to its departure, with future postmarks, and for future sales.

Inquiries to the Kniga office brought a reply from the Director-General of the Soviet export firm that "the covers are pure fakes and have never been offered by us." Mr. Belostotsky further states that there is only one MIR canceling device, and that this one has been on board the MIR space station since November 1988. He goes on that "it looks like someone has used this device for other 'black market' business, and 'that an official internal inquiry has been initiated'."

Based on this letter from the Soviet official, it appears that the covers were prepared by someone without official authorization, but that the person must have had direct access to the MIR postal canceling device either through post office or Kniga connections.

Perhaps the official investigation was successful since no further covers have been reported since this event.

Bibliography:

McMahan, Jack. 1972. *Philatelic History of Conquest of Space.* published by the author: Houston, TX.

Ramkissoon, Dr. Reuben and Lester E. Winick. 1986. *A Philatelic History of Space Exploration.* Published by the authors: Chicago, IL.

Winick, Lester E. 1978. *Soviet Space Catalog.* Published by the author: Chicago, Illinois.

Astrophile, Bi-monthly periodical of the Space Unit, Marathon Shores, FL.

Weltraum—Philatelie, e.V. Stempelforschung 81.35. "Neues über 'Kosmische Post'."

Les Winick is President of the Collectors Club of Chicago and President Emeritus of the Space Unit. He was Executive Director of AMERIPEX '86, the international stamp exhibition, held in Chicago in 1986, and served two years as a member of the Board of Directors of the American Philatelic Society. A noted author and columnist in the philatelic press, his collecting interests include astrophilately, aerophilately, as well as Iceland philately.

17

Fédération Internationale des Sociétés Aérophilatéliques, FISA — today

by **Roland F. Kohl**

FISA, the International Federation of Aerophilatelic Societies, was founded in Strasbourg, France, in 1960, but the desire for an "umbrella organization" in which all airmail collectors would be united goes back much further. As early as 1933, during the now famous WIPA exhibition in Vienna, Austria, plans were discussed to organize an "International Union of Airmail Societies." A few years later, World War II put an end to all international contacts.

Airmail collectors wanted to have a stronghold as they been receiving inappropriate treatment at exhibitions. In those days only traditional philately was recognized as "worthy of collecting." Airmail exhibits were accepted in many exhibitions, but they did not receive proper awards. A few all-airmail exhibitions (1930 in Paris, 1932 in Danzig) were organized by airmail enthusiasts with great success.

Airmail collectors from Belgium, France, Holland, Austria, Switzerland, Spain, and Germany assembled at an airmail exhibition in Wuppertal, Germany, in 1951. A document was signed by the attending aerophilatelists stating that the undersigned pledged to work on the foundation of an international organization in which all aerophilatelic societies would be united.

Dr. Jan Boesman of the Netherlands, a famous balloon pilot, was elected as President of this new body which received the name of "Fédération Internationale des Sociétés Aérophilatéliques" or "FISA." The first FISA Congress was held in The Hague in 1961 (Figure 1).

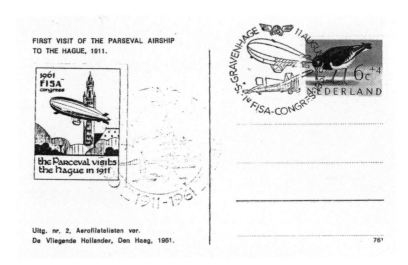

Figure 1: Post card from the first FISA Congress in The Hague, Netherlands, in 1961.

In the following years, three FISA Congresses were held in the United States: in 1966 in New York; in 1986 in Chicago during AMERIPEX '86; and most recently at CHICAGOPEX '92. The CHICAGOPEX show, significantly, was the first all-airmail exhibition sanctioned by the American Philatelic Society.

Dr. Boesman passed away in December 1976, and Roland Kohl of Switzerland was elected his successor. Within a short time of its founding, FISA achieved world-wide recognition. Aerophilatelic clubs on all five continents have joined FISA. Perhaps unavoidably, the success of FISA, which also began to give its patronage to aerophilatelic exhibitions, was looked upon with suspicion by the Fédération Internationale Philatélie, FIP. In spite of many talks between the two organizations, an agreement could never be reached. President Ladislav Dvoracek took over the helm of FIP in 1981. He not only recognized FISA's merits over the years but extended his friendship. Since that time, relations have improved and cooperation in working out new exhibition rules has been established.

Figure 2: Cover from the 26th FISA Congress during AMERIPEX '86 in Chicago, Illinois.

FISA continues to seek improvement of world-wide aerophilately. A few dedicated people meet several times during the year to discuss what can be done to promote our hobby. An exhibit has been prepared which shows the development of airmail collecting, reflected in the history of FISA. An aerophilatelist is chosen every year who is honored with the "FISA Medal." The FISA literature medal is awarded to the author of a new aerophilatelic book or catalogue. The FISA *Bulletin,* published three times a year, reflects the events and activities of our member clubs.

The work of FISA and its member societies continues to promote the significance, fascination, and challenge of aerophilately—in our eyes, the most rewarding hobby of all.

Roland F. Kohl is president of the International Federation of Aerophilatelic Societies (FISA); he has played a significant role in the promotion of our hobby throughout the world in this role since 1976. He has written and translated numerous articles in aerophilatelic journals and has a regular airmail column in the *SBZ.* He has served as editor-in-chief of the *Schweizerisches Luftpost-Handbuch* for many years and is currently Director of Foreign Relations for the American Air Mail Society. Kohl was president of the Schweizer Luftpost Sammler Verein, is an international judge and has organized aerophilatelic exhibitions.

Interested in knowing more about the American Air Mail Society and its publications? Just write to

The American Air Mail Society
Post Office Box 110
Mineola, New York 11501
United States of America

(logo taken from The *Airpost Journal* 1930 and 1931 issues)